Real Aussies Drive Utes II

Angus&Robertson

An imprint of HarperCollins*Publishers*

Angus&Robertson

An imprint of HarperCollins*Publishers*, Australia

First published in Australia in 2001
ABN 009 913 517
A member of the HarperCollins*Publishers* (Australia) Pty Limited Group
www.harpercollins.com.au

Compilation copyright © Bluey's Ute World Pty Limited 2001

HarperCollins*Publishers*

25 Ryde Road, Pymble, Sydney, NSW 2073, Australia
31 View Road, Glenfield, Auckland 10, New Zealand
77–85 Fulham Palace Road, London W6 8JB, United Kingdom
Hazelton Lanes, 55 Avenue Road, Suite 2900, Toronto, Ontario M5R 3L2
and 1995 Markham Road, Scarborough, Ontario M1B 5M8, Canada
10 East 53rd Street, New York NY 10022, USA

National Library of Australia Cataloguing-in-Publication data:

Real Aussies drive utes II
ISBN 0 207 19963 9
1. Pickup trucks – Australia. 2. Australian wit and humor.
I. Bryant, John Richard, 1946– . 3. Australia – Social life and customs.
629.28432

Cover and internal design by Judi Rowe, HarperCollins Design Studio
Cartoons by Paddy O'Leary
Printed in Australia by Griffin Press on 90gsm Econoprint

5 4 3 2 1   01 02 03 04

Contents

The Great Aussie Performer

IT WAS 11 PM ON a Saturday night when he strode into the trendy, inner-city pub in Darlinghurst. He had come from out bush — driven all night from his property near Lightning Ridge to the big smoke for his best mate's engagement party. But he was late. Bloody late.

Standing bronzed and rugged by the bar, he looked around for his mates and ordered a VB with a slow drawl.

She stood five foot nine near the bar, long and slender and clutching her designer cocktail in a taloned grip. Wearing skin-tight black — the uniform of the Darling herd — she could have easily been the queen of the scene. But something was astray. Bored insane by the elite circle of bespectacled postmodernist art critics surrounding her, she flicked her eyes around the room. Within a few dissatisfied seconds, they landed on him.

He seemed to her like a savage from the wilderness. Compared with the well-groomed male poodles of the yuppie scene he was a rottweiler, raw and brutish. She could see hair and muscle under the loose collar of his checked shirt. Furrows creased his weather-beaten face. Sun-bleached red hair fell out from under his Akubra. Pheromones wafted from his every pore. The skin on the back of her neck started to crawl. Her head swam. She leaned back on her bar stool to keep her balance, unable to tear her eyes away.

'She's a bloody sort!' he thought to himself smugly, feeling her gaze searing him. He stared back at her unabashed. Her long legs wobbled in their stilettos.

This had happened to other city girls before. He'd been told it was his 'animalism'. Apparently it was something about the way he smelled. He wasn't quite sure what that meant, but he knew it could lead to a bloody good time if he played his cards right. And considering his best mate was probably having a blinder at some strip show by now, he figured he might as well try and get some payback for the long drive here.

Her heart thundered loudly as he swaggered towards her, schooner in hand. Sparks flew as they faced each other for the first time.

'You're lookin' a bit thirsty,' he said, grinning, and he eased her near-empty cocktail glass out of her manicured grip. 'What's ya poison?'

Her refined social circle halted their debate on Far Eastern Post-structuralism, turned and gaped.

'Margarita,' she said in a trembling voice, as she steadied herself on the bar stool.

'Not ya name, girl!' he chuckled. 'Whaddaya drink?'

'Just get me a VB,' she whispered.

In a few moments he returned with her beer, thankful that the bar was closing soon, 'cause he only had a fiver left in his wallet.

'I'm actually called Monique,' she panted, intoxicated by his scent. 'And you're obviously not from around here.'

'I'm from Lightning Ridge,' he said. 'But you don't ask nobody's name up there.'

As they stared at each other, the noise and lights seemed to melt away. She abandoned her classy demeanour and gulped down the beer in seconds. The alcohol seeped into her bloodstream and she was powerless to resist his magnetism.

There was nothing more to be said. When the bar closed at midnight, they left together — swiftly.

'We can't go back to my place,' she said, as they streaked into the warm night with mutual urgency. 'Are you staying somewhere?'

His shadow fell across the dirt and cigarette butts as he paused at the street corner, contemplating the situation. Five bucks might get you a room at the pub in Moocooloola but it wouldn't go far in the bright lights of flashy Sydney.

He screwed up his face as he thought. Then he took her hand. 'I've got a car,' he said, leading her down a side lane.

The light from the street lamps struggled against the gloom of the night as the would-be lovers hurried towards their destination. In a flash they arrived, panting from the physical exertion and the promise of what was to come.

'Is that really yours?' she purred, pointing a shaking finger at the silver Porsche gleaming before them. He kissed her feverishly on the lips and felt her body go limp in his arms.

'No way baby,' he drawled, spinning her around to face the other way. 'Mine's the beast over there.'

'Oh my God! It's a *ute*!' she cried, growing weak and turning ghostly pale.

His rumbling laugh penetrated her hazy consciousness. 'Never been laid in a ute before? You call yourself an Aussie?'

He kissed her again and then with powerful arms swept her into the back — on top of a tarp, and next to the spare tyre and his faithful mongrel. The cattle dog woke up and barked a greeting.

'G'day, Blue!' he chortled, jumping in beside her. 'Keep it down will ya, mate!'

The humidity in the summer air mingled with the sweat of their bodies as the couple indulged their lascivious urges under the moon in the deserted lane. Watched only by a few transient cats slinking by, they devoured each other, consumed by intense desire. Finally, after the passion had reached its ecstatic climax, Monique wilted beside her rugged, outback lover, her head still spinning.

'That was amazing,' she slurred, letting her head fall against his rippling, hairy chest. He grinned to himself with smug satisfaction and ran a leathery hand down her smooth thigh.

'Well, ya can't beat a true blue Aussie, now can ya, girl?'

She propped herself up and looked directly in his face. 'No, stupid! I mean I've got to get one of these incredible utilities!'

The man from Lightning Ridge's jaw dropped open. Shaking his head he pulled on his jeans, slapped on his Akubra and got out his wallet. 'Tell 'em I sent ya,' he growled, handing her a business card emblazoned with: 'Moocooloola Circle Workers, Home of the Great Aussie Performer'. Then he got into the cabin, revved up the engine, waited till Monique had climbed out onto the footpath clutching her clothes and screeched away from the kerb.

He faced a long drive back up to the Ridge, but there was no place like home. City folk were just too damn weird for him.

'Oh my God! It's a ute!'
she cried, growing weak and
turning ghostly pale.

Hot Wired

A DAY AFTER THE RAIN. The paddocks are running with water and the yard is a bog. What are we going to do to fill in the time till the sun shines again?

I know. Let's go over to Gary's and we can rip around his bottom paddock in that old HK ute he's got that's not registered! We can do all sorts of things, like slides and doughnuts and spinouts and that sort of caper.

Chris and I head on over to Gary's and it doesn't take much convincing to get him to take the old ute out of the back shed. The battery is a bit flat, but the three of us push start her and when she roars into life Chris and myself jump into the back and we're sitting on this bale of hay and Gary is fairly up it, full bore down to the bottom paddock.

Neat slide, Gary. Wow. Give her more, mate. See if you can fishtail her. Beauty, cobber. What a ripper three-sixty. Oh mate, this is tops! Flatten her, Gaz, and see how far we can slide. Go, go, go. Anchors out slide, slide sliding, still sliding, sliding, straight into . . . the electric fence. You know the type. Four strands of wire, the top one is the hot one and every six metres or so is one of them wooden spacers.

The ute hits the fence and it moves upwards, the bumper goes under the bottom wire and the whole bloody lot goes up onto the bonnet, up past the windscreen. The wipers went missing some years ago. Over the cabin, and I copped it in the gob and Chris got belted in the chest.

Well, it flattened both of us. Set us on our bums across this bale and jammed us there. That flaming wire was as tight as any bloody guitar string and we were stuck there, and every four seconds ...

WHACK. 1, 2, 3, 4 ... ZAP ... 1, 2, 3, 4 ... WHACK

Come on, you mongrel ... ARGH, Gary, for ^*$^%@# sake move the ... ARGH ... c'mon you *%&^@# ... GARY, ARGH.

We're getting fried in the back and he doesn't care, does he? If the truth be known he knows exactly what's happening but he can't stop laughing, can he? He's literally rolling round the floor of the ute!!

We finally got mobile again and went back up to the house and put the ute away. Then we grabbed Mr Flamin' Hilarious and tied the mongrel up facing the strainer at the gate inside the PODDY calves' yard, slopped molasses all over him and ... see how long you laugh now, MATE!

Anchors out slide, slide sliding,

still sliding, sliding, straight into ...

the electric fence.

The Sloth

THE SLOTH IS ABOUT THE weirdest ute driver I've ever met.

Me and the Sloth drive escort utes for heavy haulage trucks, almost always at night when there's no traffic. We work under contract for a large machinery supplier, and any time they want to move their bulldozers or tractors me and the Sloth drive the escort vehicles. You may have seen us. Yellow flashing lights on top of our Falcon utes, with 'Wide Load' signs and all that sort of stuff. Usually I go out the front, with the Sloth coming up behind the low loader. We talk all the time on the CBs, warning each other and the low loader driver about approaching traffic. The Sloth doesn't actually talk, he has a sort of a grunt language that only me and some of the truckies can understand. The noise he makes on the CB is probably an echo caused by the Coke bottle that is usually in his mouth.

I'm a pretty average bloke, in that while I usually drive at night, I try not to sleep all day. The Sloth is different. Ever since I've known him, he sleeps all day and only comes out at night, sort of like a wombat or something. I doubt the Sloth has seen daylight for years, because if ever we're on the road towards dawn, he's desperate to either head for home or pull off the road and sleep. I once had a dream that he turned into an overstuffed turkey when the sunlight hit him ... maybe he would.

The Sloth has chucked the passenger seat from his XH Falcon ute so he can sort of twist himself into a sleeping position whenever he's not actually driving. I can't figure this out. I have a canopy on the back of my ute and it's set up for sleeping, with a mini fridge and stereo. The Sloth said that set-up wouldn't suit him because he'd get sick of walking from his ute door to the back of the ute, and back again. Yeah, I suppose it's a long walk!

We often spend a lot of time stopped at night, like while the Scalies (Roads and Traffic Authority) are weighing the low loader, or when the coppers are booking it. The Sloth can slip into a deep sleep in under five seconds, regardless of what's happening. One night the low loader got stuck under a bridge and pulled down some power lines, and while everyone else was watching the sparks and the frantic actions of the State Emergency Service and fire-brigade crews, the Sloth slept on.

We reckon that the Sloth must weigh over 150 kilos. He lives on a diet of Coke and chips. He's so overweight that he hardly ever gets out of his ute. He buys all his Coke and fries at drive-throughs, and I'm sure if ever they shut down the Sloth would die of malnutrition, except that it would take a long time because he has a lot of fat stored up in his tremendous gut.

The Sloth has some disgusting habits, too. Like he'll hardly ever leave his ute to visit the men's. He just does it in empty Coke bottles while sitting in his ute, and then lobs the 'fulls' into roadside bins. At least he's improved from when he used to do it onto the road. He used to simply stop his ute, swivel one leg out of the door, and pee from a sitting position. You could always see where the Sloth had been: wet patches of bitumen every 100 miles or so in the middle of the road.

Although he only grunts while driving escorts, I know the Sloth is really proud to drive a ute. The boss once suggested that he'd trade in our utes for a couple of those small Jap vans to save on fuel, and the Sloth nearly went off his head. He reckoned that real Aussies didn't drive Jap vans, and that he for one would go on strike if he ever lost his XH. It had the most comfortable seat in the world, he said. I've only ever seen the Sloth's ute seat once and it was a mess, completely collapsed from excessive driver weight. It happened when the Sloth had to leave the ute while it was being repaired. He'd dropped a French fry when leaving the drive-through one day. He slammed on his brakes and backed up to pick up the fry, and he ran into another vehicle. The Sloth believes even one fry is worth backing up for!

Because of all the time we spend together I reckon the Sloth would be one of my closest mates. Not that I really know him. He's a real loner. Come to think of it, I don't even know if he has a real name.

Probably the main thing we have in common is that we both drive XH utes ...

Beached Ute

MATE, I'VE GOT A CRACKER. It involves myself, a few of my mates and my 1995 VRII ute.

It was about four months ago when four of my mates went across to Port Macquarie from Wee Waa to escape the floods and get on it for a couple of days. I decided to meet them up there, as I was living in Sydney, having previously lived in Wauchope for fifteen years on a dairy farm.

Anyway, after going out the first night we decided that a 'bender' was due and it was our duty to go out and make absolute idiots of ourselves, which we did. Our night finished at about 3.30 am and we all made our way back to the house.

This is where it gets very interesting. The house we were staying at was right on the beach. Very nice, really. As we all arrived back, one of my mates who is a diabetic decided that he needed to go for a run to get the grog out of him, because diabetics and piss don't go well together. We all said, 'Yeah, that's fine', but when he hadn't returned an hour later we got worried. A mate and myself thought that he could have passed out on the beach.

Being the smart buggers that we are we got in my ute and drove it up onto a little cement ramp that goes down to the beach so we could shine the spotties on the sand to find our mate. Well, Tom wasn't there at all . . .

Now, here was our problem. Being a little under the weather I didn't realise it but, as I tried to do a three-point turn, I had driven the ute just a little bit too far and my rear wheels were actually off the cement and in the sand. Needless to say, we were stuffed . . .

I got out and started pushing while my mate was driving … First mistake, he put the ute in reverse, not first. We rolled backward and now all four wheels were in the sand. Now we were really stuffed. After trying for about twenty minutes with just the two of us, we realised that we needed the other two blokes. My mate ran up and got them while I sat in the ute shitting myself, worried that the cops would come and find my ute parked on Lighthouse Beach … Not good, eh!

Anyway, the fellas turned up and we all started pushing. Inch by inch we got the ute further towards the cement ramp. To make matters worse, my Ute has a stereo system in it and at four in the morning it is bloody loud. After trying for about an hour and a half and moving the car about four metres it was decided that we needed something to put under the wheels. I straightaway got the rubber tray mat out of the back and jammed it underneath. After pushing and pulling for another two hours, we finally got the bloody thing out.

You can imagine the sight … six pissed blokes trying to push a Commodore ute off a beach at four in the morning is a bloody funny thing. Later in the morning I went down to check out the damage and only then realised how dumb we'd been. The windows had been down in the ute and being rear-wheel drive and in reverse I think there was half the sand on Lighthouse Beach in the cabin. Unbelievable — there was sand everywhere. But hey, at least we got out of it safely.

To add to this, we did actually find the mate we were looking for in the first place. He had passed out in a bus shelter about ten metres from the house.

You can imagine the sight ...
Six pissed blokes trying to push
a Commodore ute off a beach at
four in the morning is a bloody
funny thing.

 Scrap Metal

ONE OF MY MATES HAD gone to a B&S and had a couple of drinks with the boys, as ya do. The night was getting on and one of the other lads there had just bought himself a brand new ute and he wanted to give her a bit of a show-off to everyone.

So he started ripping up the paddock with a bit of circle work, and he was quite proud of what she did. But this mate of mine, being the kind of bloke he is, decided that he could better that effort and took his HT ute out for a bit. So away he went, cutting sick all over the paddock.

He eventually got a bit ahead of himself and decided that he would try and get the HT airborne. Well, he sure did that all right. The old girl didn't know what had hit her. At one stage the bonnet was pointing towards the sky, and then it seemed to change directions and it was heading towards the ground at a pretty hefty speed. Luckily the ute wasn't hurt and neither was my mate, but the old HT now goes a lot faster, because when she landed the bull bar fell off.

But some good did come out of that night. He sold the mangled HT bull bar to the other lad that was doing the circle work, whose dad owned a scrap metal yard back in town. It wouldn't have been much good as a bull bar after that!

The Stiff

UP NORTHERN TERRITORY WAY THERE are a few whistle stops that masquerade as 'townships' as you drive north up the main bitumen from Alice Springs to Darwin. They usually feature a general store with a post office agency and maybe a house or two, and a couple of shipping containers doubling as sheds.

I was heading up to Jabiru via Darwin one time, and stopped at one of those small-town general stores for a cold drink. As I walked around the shop savouring the air-conditioned comfort I spied these long, weird, meaty-looking things in the freezer display case.

'What are those?' I asked the shopkeeper. 'Skinned and frozen 'roo tails,' he said. 'The local indigenous population buy them. At $2.50 a piece it's easier than hunting 'roos.'

The shopkeeper explained that these frozen 'roo tails were famous round those parts; in fact they had entered into local legend. He then told me the story that had generated the legend.

A year back the local butcher had had a load of these frozen goodies in the back of his ute on his way to deliver them to the general store, and had stopped at the pub for just one very quick drink. While he was in the pub a fight had broken out. After landing a few good right hands, the publican had managed to get the combatants out of the pub and onto the footpath.

By that time the local cop had arrived, and was standing on the edge of the crowd trying to figure out which of the fighters was buggered enough to be arrested without being able to do him any damage. Just as he'd picked out his man, his man copped a head in the stomach and lurched back against the side of the butcher's ute. Spying the solid 'roo tails, he grabbed one, deciding he could wield it like a baseball bat and turn the odds back in his favour.

With a wild yell, his man swung the frozen 'roo tail in a great arc, intending to send the head-butting scumbag to the Promised Land. At that very instant the scumbag was decked by another bloke from behind, leaving the frozen 'roo tail with a lot of momentum and no legitimate target.

Well, it's a shame that the copper was standing so close to the action. The frozen 'roo tail completed its arc, and decelerated rapidly as it came to rest on the bridge of his not inconsiderable red nose. The cop didn't know anything about it for an hour, as he was knocked cold and taken to the hospital for treatment.

Funny part of the whole deal was that the cop scrambled out of hospital and arrested his man, charging him with 'assaulting a police officer'. To complete the arrest and make the charge stick he had to impound the frozen 'roo tail, which, after being thawed then refrozen, sat curled up in the police station freezer for two months, awaiting presentation to the travelling magistrate as 'evidence'.

'If that bloody butcher carried his meat in a van like everyone else this would never have happened, and my nose wouldn't have a double bridge. Health Department ought to create a law against carrying frozen 'roo tails in the backs of utes!' said the copper. He said this every time anyone mentioned 'roos, pubs, fights or utes.

'Health Department ought to create a law against carrying frozen 'roo tails in the backs of utes!'

Beating the Breathalyzer

I'VE GOT THIS BUNCH OF mates who always go to B&S balls as a group. If one can't go, then no one goes. And when we all go anywhere, we have all these routines that keep us laughing from the time we take off till the time we get home.

One of the best stories about our B&S group happened back just after drink-driving became a big issue with the country police.

We were all at this B&S ball in a New South Wales country town, and a police patrol had parked just down the road from the hall to catch anyone silly enough to drink and drive. The copper was one of those types that must've had a miserable childhood himself, because he seemed to hate to see young people having a good time and was overzealous in nailing anyone who stepped out of line.

Late in the evening the police officer noticed a man leaving the hall so intoxicated that he could barely walk. The man stumbled around the car park for a few minutes, with the officer quietly observing. After what seemed an eternity of trying his keys on four or five vehicles, the man managed to find his ute. He got the door open, then stumbled around trying to figure out which leg to put into the ute first. He fell over twice before he finally climbed into the cabin. He was there for a few minutes as a number of other blokes and girls left the hall and drove off.

Finally this bloke started the ute, switched the wipers on and off (it was a fine, dry night), flicked the indicators on, then off, tooted the horn and then switched on the lights. He flicked up to high beam then back to low beam, and turned the lights off and then on again. He moved the vehicle forward a few inches, reversed a little and then remained stationary for a few more minutes as some more vehicles left. At last he pulled out of the car park and started to drive slowly down the road.

The police officer, having patiently waited all this time, now started up the patrol car, put on the flashing lights, promptly pulled the man over and carried out a breathalyzer test.

To his amazement, the breathalyzer indicated no evidence of the man having consumed any alcohol at all!

Dumbfounded, the copper said, 'I'll have to ask you to accompany me to the police station. This breathalyzer equipment must be faulty.'

'I doubt it,' said the man. 'Tonight I'm the designated decoy.'

'Tonight I'm the designated decoy.'

You Wouldn't Read About it!

YOU WOULDN'T READ ABOUT IT! Some time ago a mate and I decided to go pig shooting out around the Pilliga scrub. We decided to leave after work on the Friday and share the driving through the night. Well, I should have seen the writing on the wall, but this is what happened.

I was driving trucks for a living at the time, and I went to work that Friday morning and found I had a stack of drops all around the city and suburbs. I was carrying steel mesh for concreting and the like, and my first drop was over at Palm Beach in Sydney's northern suburbs. I found the address and as I backed the truck up this bloke's driveway I felt the truck drop into a hole and get bogged down. I had broken through his new concrete path and had the back wheels firmly stuck in a cavity beneath, so I had to find a tow wagon big enough to move me and one that was available straightaway.

Three hours later one rolls up and pulls me free. I gave the owner of the demolished driveway my particulars and quickly took off, trying to make up the lost time. The day went from bad to worse. Anyway, I finally got back to the yard about six that evening and was feeling pretty knackered, but at least my mate could take over driving when I picked him up.

Unfortunately, when I got to his place he was out to it on the couch — thinking I wasn't coming, he had consumed most of the slab we had bought for the trip. Anyway, I loaded him into my trusty VC Valiant ute and headed for the mountains, having to stop on the way to pick up some bullets for my new Ruger. So I lobbed into Penrith, where there was a Mick Simmons store in those days that stayed open late on Fridays, pulled over and ran into the shop. After waiting for some old bloke who couldn't make up his mind I finally got my shells. Coming back to the vehicle I found a parking ticket under the wipers, for parking in a bus stop.

Anyway, after driving all bloody night we finally reached the Pilliga. As we stopped to walk around I noticed that the wide tyres I had on the beast had effectively sandblasted all the paint off the sills of the VC. Still, we soldiered on, and finally started to do some shooting. I was real proud of my new Ruger automatic, the first one I had ever owned.

The dogs had been after the pigs near the creek and one of the buggers was heading my way. As he broke through the long grass he had an ear hanging off from the dogs and he was none too happy. He sighted me and came at me. I aimed, pulled the trigger, and then the dreaded CLICK ... nothing! I had to act quick, because this mad pig was just about on top of me. I grabbed the rifle by the barrel and coshed the porker over the head. I stopped the bugger, but broke the butt of me new rifle as well. Smart move, eh?

Later on I tried to use my long-barrelled revolver, but after nearly shooting one of the other fellas decided to leave it in the back of the ute. But THERE'S MORE ...

After a bloody waste of time and money of a weekend we finally decided to head home. However, the bloke in the local service station wouldn't sell us any fuel because we had bought a couple of Koori fellas a few beers, and afterwards one of them rode this little pony through the local grocery store as he did his shopping. But these fellas were good blokes, and came to the rescue with a 40-gallon drum of fuel from somewhere. We filled up the VC and the jerry and took off down this short cut they told us about. The road was pretty rutted, so I was doing over 100 kilometres an hour when I came around this corner slightly sideways and saw that the road was cut by a wash-out. It was too late to brake, so I planted it in the hope of jumping the gap ...

Well, almost made it: the front wheels hit the edge, which splayed them like a skier going downhill. But the worst damage was to the fuel tank, which was lying on the road a few yards back. We used a bit of bush ingenuity and tied the fuel tank to a roof rack and used an old siphon (a bit of rubber garden hose) from the fuel line to the carby. The stench of petrol was overwhelming and after a few miles, with a ute that didn't want to steer any more, we both got these enormous headaches.

We finally made into some town and were able to buy more fuel, and sure enough it started to rain. Couldn't shut the windows because of the stink, so we battled on. I forgot to mention that our little flying stunt had knocked the headlights out of whack, so every truck and most cars down the highway gave me a display of their high-beam power.

By the time I got home I was soaking wet, my head was pounding like a drum and my eyes were about the size of 20 cent pieces. My missus wouldn't speak to me, so I slept the rest of the night on the couch. I also got a serious dose of the flu and wasn't able to go to work for a couple of days.

My boss rang and said I had to come in, so I dragged myself off to work. I went into his office and he showed me the bill he copped for the bloke's driveway and promptly gave me the sack!

I said you wouldn't read about it but now you have and all the above is true. It actually did happen . . . pretty funny, eh?

Love Hurts!

BELLE FELL IN LOVE WITH Rory at first sight. She fell hard and fast, instantly infatuated the first time she laid eyes on him. Her girlfriends were really envious because she was so sure of her feelings so quickly. They asked her what was the big attraction. Deep down she knew, but to be honest she was too embarrassed to tell them. She couldn't bring herself to put it into words. Fact was, it all started long before she even met Rory.

Rory drove a slightly used Hilux ute. It was an '87 dual cab with five on the floor and 329 000 on the clock. He did all his own work on the ute, which was the only reason it still ran. That's not to say it was an unreliable ute; it wasn't. But you just needed to know which panel to bang, which wire to tug or which screw to tighten to make it start or stop or whatever.

It seemed whenever Rory worked on his ute, or anything else for that matter, he managed to inflict an injury on himself. Like one time when he replaced the Hilux's wiper rubbers, and he almost slashed his finger to the bone with his Stanley knife. When rotating his bald tyres the jack slipped and the tyre lever broke off the top of one of his two front teeth. Another time he was lying underneath the ute inspecting the holes in his exhaust system, and he managed to get dirt in his left eye, resulting in a trip to hospital to get it cleaned. He once got concussed when he caught his foot on the top of the tailgate while leaping out of the tray; he hit his head so hard on the grass that he passed out for a few seconds. 'Not the first time anyone was knocked cold by grass,' said his old man with a twinkle in his eye, hoping desperately that someone would catch his pathetic double meaning.

But perhaps the most significant and most painful injury ever suffered related to Rory's altercation with the Hilux's radiator.

Rory used to cart the most outrageous loads of stuff in his ute, and it was prone to overheating, especially on hot summer days. Being an ex-Boy Scout, Rory used to carry a 20-litre plastic drum of water in the back for whenever the radiator boiled. He knew the radiator leaked and that it probably needed flushing, but he doubted whether he could stand the injuries that such a repair job would inflict. Instead, he just waited until she boiled, then after a while he'd ease off the radiator cap and fill her up with cold water. He'd always keep the motor running so as not to allow the cold water to crack the overheated block.

Well, one hot summer's day Rory had a huge load on board. Paul, a mate, had talked him into using the ute to carry a load of ice for the local B&S ball, which was on that very night. They had loaded a small (but quite heavy) refrigeration unit onto the ute. They loaded it *onto* and not *into* the ute, because the refrigeration unit was too large to sit down on the floor, so they tied it down on the top rails, where it caused precarious swaying of the ute due to the high centre of gravity. The unit was filled with ice, and the load was way beyond safe loading limits.

As they approached the B&S venue, the poor old Hilux was labouring in third and started to boil. Paul didn't want to stop, because they were running late and the ice was melting. Rory knew that if he just kept going the ute might go off like a bomb.

'We'll pull over for a few seconds and ram some water into the radiator,' said Rory.

'Well, bloody hurry up, mate, we don't want this load of ice to turn to water before we can plug the fridge into the mains.'

Rory pulled off the road next to an old fence. He lifted the bonnet and steam was spurting out from a couple of cracks in the radiator, as well as from underneath the cap. 'Never seen her this hot before,' Rory moaned.

Rory was in favour of letting her cool off a bit to allow the steam pressure to subside, but Paul was impatient. After a short argument, Rory decided he'd better get the cap off pronto and throw some cool water down the Hilux's parched throat. Looking around the ute, he didn't have a rag to use as an insulator to protect himself from the steam, but he had a bright idea instead.

Climbing up onto the top of the adjacent post-and-rail fence, Rory balanced himself and placed his left foot down onto the radiator cap. 'Should be OK if I just ease her off,' he thought to himself. 'I can hold the cap down with me foot until some of the pressure escapes.' He was wearing a pair of pretty heavy-duty Redback boots with steel toecaps, so how could he get hurt?

As he stood down and twisted the cap, it let go under the enormous pressure of 100 cc of water boiling at a million degrees! The cap slewed sideways, and Rory's foot slipped off the radiator. A geyser of steam and boiling water shot skyward, straight up the left leg of Rory's shorts, knocking Rory off the fence and into the grass.

As he lay there clutching his groin, Rory's life flashed before him, and he entered into the true, awful and indescribable experience of Pure Pain. He'd had his balls knocked, kicked, ground and punched before in earlier accidents, but never before had he had them braised, boiled, cooked, roasted and fried, all at the same time.

It was nearly two months after this accident, after he'd just been released from hospital, that Belle had fallen in love with Rory.

Belle will never forget it. She was sipping a lemon, lime and bitters at the local beer garden when this young man caught her eye. First of all she just saw him from the waist up as he walked along behind the hedge, heading for the beer garden gate. He appeared tall, slender and tanned, and was wearing a red and white checked shirt. He had a strange sort of swagger. Under his Akubra he also had a sort of cute grin, accentuated by his chipped front tooth.

As he swung through the beer garden gate, Belle saw Rory head-on for the first time. Below his shirt he sported a pair of tight blue Wrangler jeans, which fell away into his RM Williams boots.

However, the most stunning aspect of his appearance was that he walked with the most incredible bow-legged gait that she'd ever seen. She was swamped with thoughts of John Wayne, The Lawman, Reno, Nevada, Longhorns, Johnny Yuma, Lonesome Dove and Little Joe Cartwright, all rolled into one. She suddenly realised for the first time in her life that ever since she was a little girl she had subconsciously fantasised about being swept off her feet by her very own outback cowboy. NOW it had happened.

As they slowly got to know each other better, her outback cowboy impressed her more and more. They discussed everything as they rode around in his Hilux ute, making plans for the future. They even talked about sex once but, with tears in his eyes, Rory assured her that he was not interested, and was saving himself for marriage. He proved to her that he wasn't like all the other louts that she'd met in town. He was in no hurry to rush her into his swag in the back of his Hilux. He was a pure gentleman … he respected her as a woman and as a person … he treated her like a real lady! THIS, thought Belle, is TRUE LOVE.

Perhaps the most significant and most painful injury ever suffered related to Rory's altercation with the Hilux's radiator.

Lucky Jack

JACK WAS ONE LUCKY BASTARD.

He always had been. Jack was the guy who, back when you all wagged school, would *never* get caught. He was the bloke who, when he paid for his shout with a $20 note, got change for a $50 note. Jack was the bloke who *always* managed to return from the races not just with a profit *and* a skinful of beer, but also three or four phone numbers from some of the lovely ladies he'd met during the day, *and* get let off with a warning from the random breath-testing van parked outside.

Jack was one lucky bastard.

Anyway, one day a couple of months ago, Jack got a call from a lawyer in one of those little wheat-belt towns halfway between Perth and Kalgoorlie. Apparently some distant relative of his had died, and in his will had left his farm ute to Jack. Well, Jack had nothing specific planned for that weekend, so I gave him a lift up to check out the ute. We figured that, if worst came to worst, we could go back up the following weekend with a trailer and take it back. Either that or just tow it out to the local tip.

We followed the directions supplied by the lawyer, and found the shed behind the run-down old shack that passed for the farmhouse. Jack opened the shed and there it was. Under a sheet covered in red dust was a 1966 HR Holden ute. And she was immaculate. The blue duco was virginal, the chrome polished, the upholstery unblemished. And when I peeked under the tonneau cover, I had the feeling that I was the first person to do so since she'd left the factory all those years ago. Only a thin covering of what dust had filtered through the covering sheet, and a few spider webs in the grille. I only pretended to be surprised, because deep down I think I kind of expected this.

Jack was one lucky bastard.

Jack poked his head in the cab, and read out the odometer reading.

'Twenty thousand miles — not too bad for a thirty-five-year-old farm ute, I guess — wonder if it runs?' he asked hypothetically — sort of as if there was a chance that it might not. This is, after all, Jack that we're talking about.

Jack flipped down the sun visor, and of course the keys were there waiting for him. After checking the radiator, brake fluid, tyre pressures and all the other things that you'd hate to go wrong during a test drive, Jack hit the starter. The ute started on the first kick, almost as if she was getting impatient about stretching her legs.

A couple of laps around the yard and Jack reported back.

'No funny noises from the diff or gearbox, brakes work all right — are the headlights on? Right — I'll see ya back in town!' called Jack.

'Don't want me to follow?' I asked. I think I was more worried about *my* Ute making it back than I was about Jack.

'Nah — she's right. Catch ya at the pub later tonight, all right?'

'No worries,' I replied, and headed off back to Perth.

That night at the pub, there was no Jack.

'Probably picked up a sheila at the servo while he was topping up the tank,' quipped Tommo, only half joking. He knew, after all, that Jack was one lucky bastard. Of course, the story about the HR only reinforced his thinking.

'Hope he hasn't broken down,' mused Chuckles, the resident pessimist. 'There's a lot of nothing between towns out there. A bloke could get into some real trouble.'

'Whatever you reckon, Chuckles,' Tommo and I said in chorus for about the 20th time that evening. He'd been in fine form, forecasting anything between the End of Civilisation As We Know It and the impending crash of the Aussie cricket team (which, when you think about it, are pretty close to being one and the same thing).

By mid-week, no one had heard from Jack. It was as if he'd disappeared from the face of the earth. He wasn't at home, he hadn't showed up at work (which wasn't *that* unusual), and his mum hadn't heard from him for about three months (again, not unusual).

By the following Friday night, news of Jack's mysterious disappearance had filtered through the pub crowd. The last time he'd gone missing for this long was when he was told that Murph's wife was pregnant, and that Murph's two-year-old vasectomy had given rise to some pertinent questions. Jack was one lucky bastard. He was also pretty gullible.

Anyway, late in the Friday night session, a bloke approached us from the other end of the bar. He had evidently heard the story of Jack, his new/old ute, and how he'd disappeared. It seemed this guy was a truck driver who was down from the very same wheat-belt town where I had delivered Jack the weekend before.

During the week his mate, who happened to be the local wrecker, had mentioned in passing that he'd come across the wreck of a very recently immaculate HR ute. The odometer reportedly showed only about 20 000 miles.

My ears pricked up, and the beer-induced fog started to clear away. Tommo was first with the pertinent questions. What happened? Where was it? How bad? Any idea about the driver? It had to be the same ute, didn't it? There can't be too many like that around, can there?

'I knew it,' said Chuckles, wearing a look that somehow made him look both worried and smug at the same time — I don't know quite how he managed to do *that*.

'Sorry, mate, that's all I know,' said the truckie. 'Hope your mate's OK. Sounded like the ute was a bit of a mess, but.'

So what to do? Call Jack's mum? Call his boss? Tommo, who, it became obvious, was far more sober than the rest of us, came up with the idea of calling the hospital or ambos in the wheat-belt town. He disappeared with a pile of change to the back of the pub where the public phone was.

After about a half hour on the phone he returned. No ambulance call-outs last Saturday afternoon, no mysterious coma victims at the hospital. It was as if he'd disappeared from the face of the earth. Just at that point, the new barmaid — sorry, bar attendant — came up to us.

'You blokes are Jack's mates, aren't you?'

'Yeah,' said Tommo, a gleam of hope in his eye. 'You've seen him?'

'No,' she replied, 'but this came in the post yesterday.'

It was a postcard.

From Sydney.

From Jack.

In short, sparing you the gory details, this is what happened.

Jack crashed the ute. A combination of glare from the setting sun, a kamikaze kangaroo and curiosity regarding the top speed of a mint-condition HR ute led to its untimely demise.

Jack suffered minor abrasions and cuts, and bleeding from a cut on his scalp made him look a fair bit worse than he really was.

This was when the minibus arrived.

I can just picture Jack, face covered in claret, next to a burning HR ute wrapped around a tree, when a minibus carrying the Western Australian Women's Volleyball Team on their way to the National Championships in Sydney stop to offer assistance.

Jack is one lucky bastard.

Sole Remaining Asset

IN SEPTEMBER 2000, I FINALLY found the ultimate one-owner WB ute.

A real Granddad Special, right down to the factory-option sunvisor. After some terrible crawling to the wife, I became the new owner and it became my eighteenth Holden ute. I lavished attention upon that ute; it was my pride and joy.

Well, I came home on Christmas Day to be informed by my wife that she was leaving me. I laughed at what I thought was a fairly funny joke. I nearly died when she told me she was serious. Even more so when she blamed my WB ute obsession over the preceding twelve years as part of the problem ...

Anyway, she took the kids and the furniture and I was left with the WB, a red cattle dog and a toasted-sandwich maker. After some correspondence, I christened the ute 'Sole Remaining Asset'.

Since I was miserable and despondent, my younger sister suggested that I travel to Sydney to try my luck at the Desperate and Dateless Ball. Reluctantly, I agreed.

Travelling through the Blue Mountains en route to the big event, I got hit from behind by a tourist coach. The ute then speared across the road and was T-boned by a Hyundai ...

I eventually got home and had the insurance assessor look at the ute. He totalled the damage at $5900, but the insurance company only valued the ute at $4200. This was despite the fact that I had paid $6000 for it in September AND spent nearly $2000 on it since ...

After much haggling, I convinced them to let me retain the ute to allow me to have a mate repair it. They told me that a cheque for the difference would be forthcoming.

Hearing nothing for several weeks, I started to make a few enquiries. I found out last week that my insurance company is one of those that have gone broke . . .

What a bloody year!

Well, I came home on Christmas Day to be informed by my wife that she was leaving me … she blamed my WB ute obsession as part of the problem.

Ute Power

MY OLD MAN HAS THE most powerful ute in Australia.

He started out in life as an electrician, running in and out of farm houses, up and down power poles and sticking fuses in boxes. He stuck an un-insulated screwdriver in a fuse hole once and he swore he'd never do that ever again.

Being a sparky paid the bills, but didn't give him much of a challenge. After a few years of being bored out of his brain, he decided to become an 'electrical expert'. He bought himself a laptop computer and developed some programs, which he used to check on other contractors' electrical installations.

He loved this new slant on being a sparky, because it allowed him to solve the problems others couldn't. He developed his programs to such an extent that big organisations started calling on him when their electrical systems went down, or when they couldn't work out why things didn't work. He'd just hook up his computer to the network and pretty soon he could suss out where the problems were.

His customers grew to love him as much as the other contractors started to hate him, because he could always detect shoddy workmanship quick smart.

During all of his electrical travels he'd always drive his Ford ute. Dad always reckoned any other brand was crap. When the new AU Falcon utes came out he just had to have one, and sure enough one day he turned up at home in an XLS eight-cylinder model with New South Wales number plates (1 AU UTE).

One day Dad discovered that with new software he could hook up his mobile phone to his laptop computer and suss out all his electrical programs from the cabin of his beloved AU ute. This meant he could dial up a customer anywhere in Australia, and sitting there in his ute he could access all their electrical systems. He was in heaven, being able to do what he loved most from his favourite location: his ute! 'And people pay me money to do all this, too!' he used to tell Mum, who was always vaguely suspicious of how all this techno stuff hung together.

Some of Dad's larger customers used to pay him a retainer to look after their lighting systems. This meant that he performed regular maintenance on their systems, all via his laptop computer and within his mobile office.

One night several years ago I went to the movies with a few mates and Dad had arranged to meet me outside and drive me home after the movie was over. Dad arrived a bit early, and was sitting parked in his beloved Ford ute with about thirty minutes to kill.

As he sat there in his ute in the dark, it occurred to him that he could use the time to crank up his laptop and undertake a little 'routine maintenance' on a couple of his interstate customers' systems. The economics appealed to him greatly; turning dead time into a productive opportunity. First off, Dad decided to test the emergency lighting at the University of Canberra, which was one of the prestige customers that always received Red Carpet treatment.

It was about 10.30 pm, and Dad was confident that the building would be empty and locked up. So there Dad was, sitting outside a movie theatre in Sydney in his Ford ute, tickling the keys of his laptop and merrily turning the lights on and off in Canberra.

He was just finishing this little maintenance exercise as I got into the ute. I was careful not to sit on the laptop, which would have earned me the death penalty. Dad was still chuckling to himself as he fired up the ute; after all, he'd done some powerfully valuable work while just killing time.

Just then the mobile phone rang. Since it was still sitting on the dash, I picked it up.

'Hello!' I chirped.

The voice on the other end sounded angry and very irritated. 'Can I speak to Trevor?'

'Actually Dad's driving at the moment, can I give him a message?' I enquired.

'Yeah, it's the Venue Manager from Canberra University here. Tell him that we've had a late night lecture series tonight, and some jerk must have broken into the building. He's been running round turning the emergency lighting on and off. I've had three blokes chasing all over the buildings trying to catch him, but he moves like greased lightning. We haven't been able to catch him yet, but when we do we'll skin the bugger alive. I need to talk to your dad about installing a security programme to stop idiots like this interrupting our activities.'

On yer Dad, another satisfied customer!

Pickup Confusion

THIS MATE OF MINE STARTED a company called 'Pickup Solutions Pty Ltd' which sold a spray-on product that protected the backs of utes. They sprayed this chemical goo about eight millimetres thick onto the load area, and this was said to prevent damage. After racking his brain for a gimmicky name, he ended up marketing the spray-on chemical under the name of 'HardWrap'. His advertising blurb read 'Let us HardWrap the back of your ute in the world's hardest protective coating.'

Pickup Solutions, like any business, was always hotly promoting its products, and a lot of the communication with its customers took place on the phone. If you ever called Pickup Solutions, chances are a bloke called Eric Munns would answer. Eric came out of retirement to work at Pickup Solutions and he'd had many years' experience in marketing, selling and customer relations. He presented an easy-going, friendly approach to anyone who called up; a real old-time gentleman! He was also a pretty keen salesman, and wasn't adverse to bulldogging the occasional customer order.

Well, business was enough of a challenge without getting involved in misunderstandings, but unfortunately everything isn't always as straightforward as it seems. One day Eric was working away at Pickup Solutions, plotting on how he could sell a few more orders of HardWrap and beat his sales target for the month, when his phone rang.

'Pickup Solutions, Eric speaking,' he enthusiastically chirped.

'Is dat da pickup place?' asked a swarthy voice with a heavy accent.

'Yes, this is Pickup Solutions, how may I help you?' replied Eric, sensing another order to add towards his monthly target.

'What sort of girls you got?' asked the voice.

'Girls? What difference does that make? All our staff are well trained and experienced and we have an excellent reputation for quality. In fact, everything is covered by a twelve-month warranty,' said Eric, a bit puzzled by such a weird question.

'No, I wanna know what sort of girls. I don't care about warranty, just girls.'

'I think perhaps you may have the wrong number,' responded Eric. He was now totally confused and wondering why anyone would care about the background of any of the staff in the factory.

'Wrong number? You said dat was da pickup place!' complained the voice, getting a bit edgy. 'What business you in?'

'We sell HardWraps,' said Eric proudly, feeling that at last he was getting the customer back on the right track.

'Hard wrap? You just sell da hard wrap? How can you make da money out of just selling da hard wraps?' asked the voice in amazement.

'I'll have you know that Pickup Solutions is the exclusive supplier of HardWrap in Australia and that we are a very successful company. Every ute needs HardWrap protection!'

'Sure, everyone needs a hard wrap for da protection, but you gotta be crazy if you think I'm gonna buy just a hard wrap without da bonk!'

Now, Eric had never heard of anyone fitting a 'bonk' to a ute. In fact he wasn't sure, but he somehow vaguely assumed that a 'bonk' was a four-wheel drive product and certainly not something sold by Pickup Solutions.

'Can I send you out a brochure? What's your address?' Eric asked. This was always his last line of defence. Whenever he felt a deal slipping away he'd try and get a name and address so he could continue the sales pitch via Her Majesty's mail.

'I don't need da bloody brochure. I use plenty of hard wraps before.'

Eric felt a glimmer of hope; he now knew he was talking to a repeat customer, the easiest of all to sell to. He started to get excited; he felt the sale was almost in the bag.

'Great, you've used HardWrap before! How did you use it? Were you satisfied with its performance? Did it provide the protection that you needed?' he asked with expectancy.

'What? You a filthy perv or sumfink? You guys must be &$#&^& crazy!'

The line went dead.

'Gees, maybe I'm slipping,' thought Eric, as he stirred his white tea with two sugars. 'It's not often I can't get a brochure into the mail.'

Ute Dog

I HAVE A SIX-YEAR-OLD border collie called Rusty. My old ute was a WB Holden. If I chained Rusty in the back, he used to hang over the side to look at me in the mirror, which he'd do for the whole trip. I only ever drove at 80 kilometres an hour with him in the back, as any faster the wind was too strong for him and he alternated between getting sand-blasted and hiding behind the cabin. If I wanted to go somewhere 'in a hurry' I let him in the front, which he loved. Given a choice, indicated by an open door, he would always get in the front.

One day I sold the WB and bought a new AU Falcon. Rusty's days in the front ended, and he was in the tray no matter the speed being travelled. Having a sharp mind, I never opened the ute door before I had him tied up in the back, especially if he had muddy paws.

One night I let him out the front door of the house for his daily 'walk 'n' sniff' and he didn't come back. Usually he'd be gone ten minutes and then scratch at the front door to come back in. I called and called and called, and walked a few of the neighbouring streets with a torch calling him to come, but couldn't find him.

The next morning I went to get in the ute to go to work, and found him huddled between the passenger seat and the firewall, wagging his tail as I got in.

I had left the driver's window down about halfway, and he had decided that next time we went somewhere, he was getting in the front!

The Falcon 4 x 4 Ute!

I'VE GOT THIS MAD MATE called Midge, who lives on a property not far from our place, out Walgett way. He's a bit of a shy bloke, but like most ute drivers he's a larrikin at heart.

Midge has two passions in life. One is Ford utes and the other is four-wheel drives. He'd been driving battered old second-hand Ford utes most of his life, but recently he'd bitten the bullet and bought himself a brand new AU Falcon ute. It'd take him six years to pay it off, but so what? He was in love!

Sitting just outside his shed Midge had another ute, an old 75 series Landcruiser with plenty of dings, full of rust, and with almost no original paint. This old girl was reserved for the rough jobs, and the new AU was kept for Sunday Best. He'd only ever drive her in the wet when he made an error with his weather predictions.

One night at the local, one of the boys said he'd been to a ute show at Armidale where someone said that Ford was going to release a four-wheel drive Falcon ute. Midge's ears pricked up. 'It'd be a bloody winner, I can tell ya. Everyone in Australia would buy it!' As Midge lay in bed that night he couldn't get the promise of a four-wheel drive Falcon ute out of his mind.

The next day he was in town picking up some photos from the one-hour shop (which had rushed his developing through in just over two days), and he spied a note on the wall that read 'Signs Made To Order'. Midge's fertile imagination rose to the fore, so he slapped his money down and ten minutes later walked out with his two new signs.

As soon as he got home he parked in his shed (away from the damaging UV rays of the sun) and circled the AU. After a lot of squinting and aligning, he stood back and admired his handiwork. There, on both sides of the cabin, just above the official Ford 'Supercab' signage, he had added '4 x 4' in the same font. So it now read '4 x 4 Supercab'.

'Brilliant!' thought Midge. 'For $11.20 I've converted her from a 2 x 4 to a 4 x 4!'

To really make her look that much more genuine, he borrowed a couple of hundred dollars from his Old Muther, and got the local suspension shop to push her up in the sky a couple of inches. Next stop was Max's Tyre Shop, where he traded in his near-new Dunlops for a set of second-hand off-roaders.

'Man,' Midge said as he stood back and sucked in his breath, 'the sucker sure looks like a 4 x 4 now!'

Well, the new signage, tyres and ride height had an immediate impact everywhere Midge went. It looked so subtle, so official, and so original that it drew a heap of stares and comments. Most blokes that saw it (but, sadly, almost no sheilas) would saunter over and say, 'I'd heard this was cumin' out; how's she handle the rough stuff?'

Midge was the sort of bloke who had never ever done anything famous before, so instead of setting people straight about his little deception he just let 'em believe what they wanted to believe. He never actually lied, of course, but he never actually told the full truth either.

Midge of course believed that his little AU 'trick' was all good harmless fun, and in a sense it was. Of course he hardly ever saw a lot of the fights that he caused in pubs, between blokes who on one hand swore they'd seen a 'factory 4 x 4 AU Falcon ute' and others who called them liars.

And he never saw that cocky in Narrandera, either.

Midge had gone to a bull sale there, and had angle-parked his 4 x 4 Supercab outside one of the pubs. He'd just had one for the road and was about to head home. He went outside, jumped into the AU, kicked her over and took off — all in one effortless single action.

He never saw the cocky that was lying underneath the rear axle, trying to suss out the mechanical mysteries of the first ever Falcon 4 x 4 ute he'd ever seen. Lucky for him, his body was dead centre under the axle between the back wheels.

'Shit, that was close,' he was heard to say, as he sat bolt upright on the tarmac and watched Midge's ute rocket off out of town. 'But I just might buy meself one of them Falcon 4 x 4s — they've plumbed it real neat — could be mistaken for a 2 x 4!'

One of Kev's Old Ewes

KEV SWITCHED HIS ALLEGIANCE SOME years back, from the Bulldogs to the Tigers. Old Bull his mascot had died and Kev himself had just gone into sheep, so he got a black kelpie and called him King. The droughts are pretty bad up Eppalock way, so he bought an old ute for carting the odd dead sheep to the tip and a galvanized grain silo to see him through the bad years. Like '97, when El Niño'd been a fair bugger, and the Tigers hadn't made it to the top of the ladder either.

He painted the silo in the Tigers' black and yellow stripes, so that from our front porch it looks as if a great bumblebee is sitting on top of the cootamundras.

Dick and I still have our weekender next door to Kev's paddock. He's a good bloke, so when he's short of grass we open up the gates and let his sheep eat out our three acres. The sheep had our place looking like green velvet last weekend, the trees all wearing short-back-and-sides, so that even if it hadn't been for the god-awful stench when I got out of the car I'd have soon noticed the dead sheep stretched out under the grevillea.

I climb straight over the fence to Kev's place with the kelpies going berserk, all stiff black bristles and white fangs. I know Kev's dogs, though. He brings them up noisy and good-natured like himself so they shut up once they recognised me and start sniffing up and down my legs to see where I've been. There's Prince, who Kev got a few years back to understudy King, and a pup just a couple of months old, but I can't see Queenie anywhere. Queenie would be in between Prince and the pup.

I can hear the footie on Kev's tellie and I wish I hadn't come.

'G'day!' he says in that kind of way that makes you feel he thinks you're a good bloke too. Kev's a man's man. Goes pig shooting. He's the sort of person who can fix engines and knock up a shed. He drives the local fire engine. He can build fences, lay concrete, and make a blast with dynamite that left Dick slathering with jealousy. Yep. Kev is a proper bloke.

'Geez, Jean,' he says to me, 'where ya been? Long time no see. How's the old man?'

'Look, I'm sorry,' I say back. 'I know the footy hasn't finished yet.'

'No worries,' he says, 'I've just turned it on and it's bloody all over bar the shouting. I forgot. I'm ironin', you see. I'll just keep on while we're talkin'. I'm a great ironer, I like ironin' everything.' He gave a good-natured belly laugh. 'Underpants, singlets, pillow slips, me sheets. The lot.'

I mention the dead sheep then and he says he'll bring round the ute just as soon as he's ironed his underpants. I ask him where Queenie is and he gives a bit of a wry cackle.

'Shot,' he says, 'chasin' me neighbour's sheep.'

'Gees,' I says to him, 'why'd you have to shoot her, mate? I'd have paid for the damage.'

'Well, I bought the pup here.'

'What's his name?' I ask, but I know of course.

'Duke,' he says, and reaches into the washing basket for his smalls.

Kev ambles round to my place fifteen minutes later and I go out with him to where the sad event has taken place.

'She'll be right, mate,' he says. 'Pheeoow, been dead a while. One of me old ewes.'

Tufts of wool are starting to drift out across the grass and crows or foxes have been at the beast's eyes. Kev bends over and lifts the carcass by its back and front legs while I watch, hypnotised in case it disintegrates and dribbles down his jeans. He lugs it on his knee to the tray of the ute and whistles up his dogs.

He props himself against the tray and stands yarning to us while hot gusts from the putrid flesh barrel up into our lungs. I stoop to scratch King's grizzled old chin. Kev grins affectionately at the old kelpie.

'I've dug his grave,' he says. We stand a moment adjusting our thinking to a statement that seems slightly indecent, callous even. 'King has slowed down but he still enjoys a wobbly piddle on the fence posts.'

He goes on, chuckling, 'Yeah, got the old dynamite out and the pick and shovel and dug a good roomy four be four. Don't want the poor old bugger cramped.'

'But what does King think of all this?' I say.

'Gees, he loves it, Jean. He hopped in and lay down. He knows it's his hole all right.'

'But Kev, you wouldn't …' I can't say the terrible words, but Kev gets my drift and is shocked.

'Geez no, Jean,' he says. 'I wouldn't do that to me old mate. Nah. You see, I worked it out this way. One of these mornin's I'm gonna wake up and find he's died during the night, and it's gunna be bad enough feelin' all choked up without havin' to dig a great bloody big hole.'

I get the point. Kev is all stubble and singlet and towelling hat on the outside, but inside he's good value.

He calls up King and Prince and Duke, and they all scramble into the back of the ute with the dead ewe. They belt round and round the tray and all over the corpse in a crazy mass of black yapping fur and wagging tails, but there's something I need to tell Kev urgently.

'Kev,' I yell as he starts up the engine, 'you won't forget to wash your hands before you cook dinner, will you?'

'No worries, mate,' he says, and hot blasts from the corpse roll over us as he swings the ute round and heads out Eppalock Road to the tip.

Wal and Les's Fishy Tale

THERE AREN'T TOO MANY PEOPLE who can claim to know Wal Piggott and Les Atkinson.

Those who do don't get five minutes of peace before hearing about the whopping great cod Wal and Les pulled from the mighty Murray back in '76. Until this very day in pubs around the country the story can be heard, and goes something like this:

The October of '76 saw the Murray run pretty high with some good rains, which not only made the cotton cockies happy, but also put a smile on the faces of Wal and his good mate Les. Wal and Les had been dreaming of catching a monster cod, but from all reports the days of these whoppers had long since passed. No such rumours were about to stop these two, however, especially since both their old ladies were busily cooking pumpkin scones for the upcoming show. Wal and Les weren't about to let a weekend of freedom slide away.

So off they set after loading up Les's FJ ute. Les loved his ute, but Wal wished he'd drop a new donk in it. Sitting on 40 miles an hour down the Newell was not Wal's idea of a good time. To ease the boredom Wal started to talk baits and rigs, which pretty much fell on deaf ears as Les had a habit of astutely listening to the chug of his beloved ute no matter how long the journey. Les used to do this with his head leaning slightly forward and tilted to the side as if the offer of his ear was comforting the old girl.

This must have gone on for about two or three hours, Wal's idle chit chat, Les's familiar pose, until a whopping great thud and flash of yellow and white bouncing off the windscreen threw Les back against the back rest and jammed his foot on the brake.

To his left was Wal, in the same position but looking markedly whiter and more shaken than his mate. A few seconds passed before Wal broke the silence. 'Cripes, Les, I think I've shat myself. What the hell was that?'

'Well, Wal, that was a sulphur-crested cockatoo,' Les stated as he anxiously struggled to find reverse gear, 'and those buggers make the best cod bait known to man!'

Wal couldn't believe what happened next. Not thirty seconds after taking this poor bird's life, Les was down on his haunches with a gleaming smile, scraping up the road kill to use for bait. At the least he could have shown a little remorse!

About four hours later, they both sat on the bank of the Murray with not a worry in the world, except for the twelve carp sitting beside them which seemed to be the only things taking a liking to the feast of earthworms and bardi grubs on offer. Wal was a good fisherman, but a slightly impatient one. These characteristics meant that he very rarely let pride get in the way of catching a fish.

'Hey, Les, how 'bout we give that galah of yours a go?'

To which Les replied, 'It's not a galah, Wal, it's a bloody white cockatoo. Big cod get spooked by any bright colours, especially pink!'

Les unwrapped the cockatoo and passed it to Wal, who proceeded to shield the bird from Les's vision as he plucked the bright yellow crest from its head. After feeding a hook through the bird he quickly tossed it into the river.

Well, this darn bird must have floated right down into the mouth of a big green cod no less than 60 pounds. Wal got the fright of his life as the monster stripped the line from him quicker than a Bemborough finish. This giant of the river struggled to carry her huge weight, however, and an experienced Wal played her out until she was too tired to lift a fin. Both Les and Wal were quivering with excitement as they struggled to drag the beast up the bank. Out of the water she was just as big as they had imagined.

Surely no one could deny them this fishing tale; the proof was right in front of them this time, and there could be no talk of the one that got away. In their haste to get to the local to show off their catch, the two proud anglers decided to head off directly, despite the beast still having a little kick left in her. Les got into action quickly after recovering his breath. He hopped in his ute and backed her as close to the fish as possible to hoist it in, without allowing the angle of the bank to hinder the FJ's take-off.

What Les had not accounted for was the fact that the slime from a 60-pound cod greatly reduced the coefficient of friction against the tray of an FJ Holden ute. With the fish in the back and a foot on the pedal, Les and Wal started to labour up the mounds and hollows of the bank. With each little bump that big fish slid closer and closer to the tailgate, before it eventually sprang the latches and hit the turf. Wal and Les heard the big thud and had just enough time to see their fish of a lifetime slide towards the water. With a weary flick of the tail, the big green beast slid gracefully into the depths of the Murray.

The tears started to well in both their eyes. Wal even desperately looked around on the offchance that someone had witnessed their awful plight, but there was no one within cooee, and surely no one was going to believe their story.

Les's shoulders couldn't slump any lower as he got out of the ute and walked towards the back. Just as he went to shut the tailgate he noticed a huge scale about the size of a beer coaster caught up in the hinge. Les let out a little chuckle at the reminder of the beast. He picked it up and off they headed. In contrast to the drive down, Wal didn't say anything on the way home, and Les couldn't have cared less about the chug of his FJ.

It took many a year for Wal and Les to get over their loss, but if you ever bump into them at the local down the Riverina way, I'm sure they'll spin you the yarn till they're blue in the face.

And before Les makes his way from the pub, just be sure to get a glimpse of what dangles from the end of his FJ's car keys. I'm sure you'll agree that huge cod scale makes a darn fine key ring and, for Les, an enduring reminder of that fateful day and of the one that got away.

Les had a habit of astutely listening

to the chug of his beloved ute …

with his head leaning slightly

forward and tilted to the side …

My 1927 Oakland Utility

SHE WAS PART OF OUR EARLY married life, our blue Oakland ute. She was born in 1927 and, like most females, she had many peculiarities.

The wheels were 23-inch disc and, as you may imagine, were quite tall. These were an advantage, as we have often bumped home on a flat tyre when we didn't have the finances to afford a spare. I would have to mend the puncture that night so I could drive to work the next morning. We also had battery problems, and many times we bumped over the rough corrugations of the gravel road switching the headlights on and off to conserve power so we could reach home, but we always made it somehow!

The clutch gave out on us another night, when Maureen was due to go into hospital to give birth to our child, but a taxi came to our rescue, which was lucky.

Then there was the time at eleven at night, after the pictures. I was cranking up the ute and the crank handle came out, catching my fingers between the crank and the angle iron of the numberplate. I hurled that crank handle about 50 yards, swearing and wringing my painful, blackened fingernails, but that was part of the prestige of being the proud owner of a ute. Some seasoned miners across at the pub who witnessed this had a good laugh, but it didn't cause them to stop drinking the amber fluid and come over to help during their merriment. No doubt the sound of the handle clank clanking along the dark roadway was the subject of many a laugh as the miners told of my misfortune at smoko time on the north Kalgoorlie shaft. My fingers were that sore, I couldn't have cared less.

It took me months and many bruised fingernails to master the technique of cranking the motor to start her up. After many breakdowns and trials, we converted the vacuum tank petrol system to gravity feed, which was a novel project for me.

My brother-in-law placed a four-gallon drum above the tray of the ute. When we filled this with petrol, the blue ute would happily churn through the miles and thirstily gulp the petrol. Then, on the advice of my comrades, we installed a Ford A carburettor for fuel economy. We got about 12 miles a gallon, maybe.

The ute went like a train on a trip we made out to Parkeston, near Kalgoorlie. We were kept busy loading the tray with old, rejected timber railway sleepers, which we chopped up later at home and used for firewood and heating purposes, as gas was not available in Kalgoorlie at that time. After we bade farewell to Parkeston we raced away towards town and the prospect of a cool Hannan's beer and a roast dinner, we hoped!

Everything was going fine until the car konked out near the top of a steep hill. I immediately thought, 'Hello, fuel blockage.' I allowed the ute to roll backwards to the foot of the hill.

I undid the two bolts of the carburettor and blew through the jets and the fuel lines to clear any obstruction. I turned on the ignition, cranked up the motor and was rewarded with instant success as it roared into life. Away we flew to the top of the hill and again the motor conked out. We rolled back to the bottom of the hill and repeated the procedure and again attacked the hill aggressively, with the same result.

The air was becoming electric with the adjectives I was using to encourage the ute to travel towards the summit of the hill. In desperation we sent a passing cyclist to enlist the help of a mechanic. He cycled away, oblivious to the frustration felt by the stranded motorists, racking their brains for a solution to their situation.

We knew that we had fuel and spark and that the fuel lines were clear. Why the hell would it konk out near the top? It was then that my travelling companion had a brilliant idea.

'Let's try going up in reverse!'

I thought maybe he was off his rocker for suggesting such a foolish idea, but at this stage I was prepared to try anything. I had to be guided up the hill, as the load of wood was higher than the cab and I had no clue as to where I was reversing to. Well, the ute absolutely sailed up the hill, without any trouble at all! The way the motor pulled, it would have done justice to Peter Brock's racing car. We met the mechanic on his way out to assist us and he was naturally concerned for our survival.

The problem had been obvious! As the flying Oakland, my pride and joy, approached the summit of Billy Goat Hill, the weight on the tray made the level of the petrol in the gravity tank lower than the carburettor, which was the same as running out of gas. Of course, when we reversed, the petrol ran down into the carburettor and the ute flew like a bird.

Well, we sped home and enjoyed the long-awaited Hannan's beer at the pub. By the time we had told and retold our frustrating and unbelievable experiences, with many embellishments and a variety of versions, we could finally see some humour in our ordeal, but there certainly had not been much joy at the time.

The ute is over seventy years of age now and I fancy her skirts would be a little dusty. A watchmaker is now the proud owner of the Oakland and she still struts her stuff around the Esperance streets.

I do hope the current owner has changed the gravity feed of the petrol and trust that Esperance has no monster range akin to Kalgoorlie's notorious Billy Goat Hill, as only Goldfields spirit, determination and Hannan's ale will overcome the kind of adversity.

Ute Travelogue – A True Story

I AM A SOLDIER IN the Australian Army. Last year I acquired my grandfather's stock HX ute.

Throughout the year, every possible weekend that I was home in Queensland I would spend on fixing the old girl up. After a few compulsory extras (five-poster bull bar, UHF, tint, side skirts, stereo and a shit load of lights) I decided the bus needed a cancer operation and a new coat of jam. I had just got all the work done to the point of the undercoating with help from a mate at work, when we were deployed to Timor over Christmas.

Upon return I had to move to Perth. So I got my shit together, finished the paint job, put her all back together and was feeling really proud. Decided that I would drive the Ute via Vic and show the grandfather how she looked. This is where the drama begins.

Day 1: Three hours out of Townsville all is well and out of nowhere 'Burt' (the ute's named after Grandfather) decided to blow his timing gear. Stuck 100 kilometres south of Charters Towers with just the UHF. A few trucks stopped and offered what they could, but truckies don't get a lot of time to bugger around. Three hours later, my Akubra proved its worth and a champion old cocky pulled over and decided that it was his mission to tow me the 260 kilometres south to Claremont. With no vacuum-assisted brakes and a 3-metre tow chain, it was a bloody long trip. Because it was a Saturday I had to spend the weekend stuck in Claremont with no car. The pub was on.

Day 3: The shops finally open and into the workshop I go. There was only one mechanic, as the other was sick, so I was shown where the tools were and did what I could, with the mech helping out when he got the chance. Timing gear, harmonic balancer, dizzy gear, sump gasket and $500 later I'm on the road again. Spent the night at Rollston Pub (great place to camp).

Day 4: Made it to Barooga (on the Murray) after a long day and engine temp problems; totalled 1700 kilometres.

Day 5: All well and good; repaired the overheating problem, and Grandfather got to see the ute and was very happy.

Day 9: Preparing to hit the road again, ducked over the river to Cobram to get some supplies and on the way back got stuck at a stop sign at some road works. Whilst at the stop sign, a Coca Cola rep comes around the corner in his nice red Camry towing a trailer. Busy eating a peach, he doesn't see me or the stop sign and *slams his car fair up my arse*! The tailgate was rooted and couldn't be opened and I felt like my heart had just been ripped out. He was kind enough to do the righty and we exchanged details.

Day 10: Hit the road for Adelaide. Engine troubles again, cough and splatter all the way there. Pulled into a servo in Adelaide and blew the carby out with compressed air. All fixed once again.

Day 11: Made it to Ceduna with no real big dramas.

Day 12: Up early the next morning to accomplish the Nullarbor and Burt won't bloody start. Off with the dizzy and the rotor button isn't even turning. Out with the dizzy, and sure enough the dizzy gear has had a brain fart. On my feet and around the shops I go, until I finally come across a joint with the part about 6 kilometres from the ute. Fitted and on the road again with no troubles for the rest of the day.

Day 13: Last day on the road; four hours from Perth and the ignition barrel decides that it wants to come loose and turn the ute off whilst in full flight. No stopping now, so I drive with my hand on the key the rest of the way into Perth. Finally get to a mate's place and decide to put Burt to rest for a few weeks, and go and pick up a second car from TNT.

Am all settled now. Coca Cola has come to the party and the ute is currently in the panel shop getting a new shit shoot (tailgate) and a bit of a nip and tuck.

Do hope that you enjoyed the read about the road trip from hell. Farewell, fellow ute lovers.

John and Liz

JOHN ROTTENBURY (REAL NAME) FROM Fair & Square Bricklaying (real company west of Sydney) drove a Holden HQ (real Aussie ute) with a Chev 351 motor (real fast) in his younger years. Although he's over thirty now and much wiser, he admits to being Young and Naive when he first started slapping mud around building sites.

Young John became infamous fairly early in his career. It started when he was working on a city building site and the concretors had just finished a big pour. The concrete had just gone off when Young John decided it was time for Lizard, his sharpai-blue heeler cross, to take a break from guarding his ute.

Lizard was some dog. He had blue eyes, blue lips, blue fur and even a blue tongue; in fact if ever a dog should have been called 'Bluey' it was this one, but Young John named him Lizard in celebration of his unique tongue.

Anyway, in his enthusiastic response to being freed from the chain in the back of Young John's HQ, Liz dashed straight through the fresh wet concrete. Young John went berserk, shouting and frothing at the mouth. Poor dog thought John wanted to play so he dashed straight back through the concrete, wrecking yet another area of the slab!

Young John's most famous exploit was at The Big Party, when a newly arrived neighbour threw a house-warming party and invited the whole district, including Young John and partner. The new neighbours were apparently incredibly wealthy (or very corrupt?), because they arranged a *pallet* of Jack Daniels, which meant The Big Party lasted several days.

During the course of The Big Party many people became somewhat extroverted, performing with the karaoke machine and doing their favourite party tricks. Young John was a quiet lad, so when it came to be his turn he just grabbed Liz and let everyone stare down his blue throat. The amazement didn't last all that long and there were suggestions that Young John needed to do a bit more to entertain the group. Liz slunk off to sleep in the back of the HQ while Young John struggled for ideas.

'OK,' said John, 'I'll jump me ute over that dam,' pointing at a small, muddy lake about half a kilometre down the back paddock.

There were wild Indian whoops and cries of 'Go Johnno!' as the HQ belched smoke and spat turf. After a few hoops, accelerating as hard as he could, Young John hit the dam wall at somewhere between 30 and 100 kilometres an hour. Eyewitnesses just couldn't agree on the speed, but they all agreed on what happened next. The HQ ramped up and flew into the air at the same angle as the dam wall: front point moon-ward, rear pointing ground-ward, sort of like a Cape Canaveral rocket stalling at the launch. The engine screamed, because Young John forgot to take his foot off the accelerator when the wheels left the ground. The HQ seemed to defy gravity and just hang there in space for a few seconds, before coming down fair in the middle of the dam. There was a huge tidal wave and lots of steam, as the HQ sank slowly to the bottom. As the wash subsided Liz was seen dog-paddling to the shore, blinking his blue eyes, with his blue tongue licking his very wet blue lips.

The crowd screamed and applauded, mostly in amazement that anyone could be stupid enough to think of such a stunt, let alone try it in his OWN ute.

In all the excitement it occurred to only one person that Young John was nowhere to be seen. A black man, who was the best horse rider in the district, sprinted to the dam and dived in, boots, clothes, hat and all. After a lot of froth and kicking he emerged next to a dazed but smiling Young John, who had his right thumb raised heavenward. The crowd went berserk, and for years afterwards everyone in the district stood in awe of Young John's breathtakingly brave but extremely stupid stunt.

When telling the story, though, Young John rarely mentions what happened *after* The Big Party. When the party cobwebs cleared, the neighbour realised that there was a rotting HQ still in the dam under water level. There was an oil slick as well. 'Pollution,' thought the neighbour. All pretence of friendliness vanished, as the neighbour demanded that Young John remove his HQ or suffer the legal consequences. After a lot of sweating Young John finally was forced to get a professional diver to come and attach chains, plus hire a crane, to remove it.

She's My . . .

I've had my share of fast cars,
Some shiny ones at that;
I've also had some other ones
That were just heaps of scrap.
I've knocked around the city
And around the bush as well,
But I was missing something,
Just what I couldn't tell;
Until one day I saw it,
Then yelled out, 'You beaut!'
For standing right before me
Was a beat-up Holden ute,
With multicoloured panels
And scratches everywhere:
Just the sort of thing you need
To take you anywhere.

I didn't show much interest —
That just isn't how it's done,
'Cause negotiatin' the better deal
Is all just part of the fun.
So we talked of fishing and football
And then I took the plunge:
I asked how much he wanted
For that heap of mobile grunge.
One thousand dollars poorer,
But gee, I'm feeling great,
'Cause I know I have found
My best and truest mate.
She's had her share of hard knocks
And got some scars to show
And heaps and heaps of rattles,
But strike me, can she go!
She uses oil like a sieve
And guzzles petrol too,
But if someone ever stole that ute
I don't know what I'd do.

We've had a lot of fun together
And our share of problems too,
But together me and that old ute
Will always see it through.
You see, she's more than just a car,
She's as tough as an old boot.
Thirty years on and still going strong:
She's my Holden ute!

Dad's You-Beaut-Ute

MY OLD DAD WAS A real bushie. He reckoned it was better to keep your mouth shut and be thought a fool than to open it and confirm the fact. When he did have something to say, it was short and to the point. I remember a bloke asking him, 'What do you call your dog, Bob?' and Dad said, 'I don't call him nuthin', he follers me.'

It was this quirk in Dad's personality that made it bloody near impossible to argue with him. But that didn't mean he wasn't disagreeable or, for that matter, crafty, shrewd, and devious.

There were several things that Dad always held sacred. One was his old Landcruiser ute, and another was his cattle dogs. The closest I ever saw Dad come to outright argument involved these hallowed two.

Dad was cursing because his cattle dog Blue was once again nowhere to be found. Dad was half a mile from his camp, searching and calling for him, when his mate Jack drove up in his Ford ute. He stuck his head out of the window and said, 'Lost something, Bob?' Dad snarled.

Next thing Blue jumped out of Jack's ute and joyfully bounded around Dad's legs. 'I picked him up at the Nine Mile,' said Jack. Dad snarled again, as he and Blue climbed into Jack's ute and headed back to camp.

'Nothin' worse than a mongrel that wanders,' Dad muttered.

'Wanders be buggered,' said Jack, 'he keeps falling off that rustbucket of yours. This is the sixth time I've picked him up in a month. If a bloke could talk sense into you, you'd get yourself a new Ford ...'

Dad gritted his teeth and said, 'A new dog's what I'm getting.'

Mrs Mavis Thwaites from Burnie Downs had pups for sale, and Dad would not be shifted from his resolve to buy one to replace Blue, there and then. Jack tried valiantly to dissuade Dad, as he quite enjoyed the established routine of picking up Blue. It had provided him with many happy hours of tormenting Dad.

'Look, Bob', said Jack, 'there's a helluva storm brewing behind Burnie Downs, and you'll kill yourself if you try and outrun it in that bloody old heap of yours.'

Dad said, 'I'm getting a dog. I'm going in me ute. She'll outrun any storm, and any bloody Ford!'

'You're on!' said Jack, waving a £20 note.

Business was never officially sealed at Mrs Mavis Thwaites' place until a nice hot cup of tea and some pumpkin scones had cemented the deal. But such was the weight of pride and competition upon Dad and Jack that good manners and the pumpkin scones were waived, and the pup was tossed into the back of Dad's ute and they bolted.

The storm was in full force as Dad streaked towards his camp, with Jack behind him at times, beside him at others, and occasionally disappearing down so-called short cuts.

Dad and Jack were neck and neck as they hurtled into the camp. Lightning split the air and lit up their eager faces. 'Ah ha,' cried Jack, triumphantly pointing to the three spots of rain on his windscreen. ' … The Ford wins. She outran the storm by the leanest margin.'

Dad said, 'Pull the other one mate. There's no rain on the Cruiser's windscreen, and look here, the puppy's drowned in the back of the ute!'

'I'm getting a dog. I'm going in me ute. She'll outrun any storm, and any bloody Ford!'

The Promise

COOKTOWN IS A DRINKING MAN'S town, par excellence. My husband and his brothers have honed this skill to a level equalling the finest neurosurgery. They are decent, hardworking Aussie blokes so I had learned to accept the Saturday Night Charade. Besides, they were cheerful drunks and entertaining in a beery, nonsensical sort of way.

This particular Saturday night promised to be quiet and domesticated until the spouse, Brother Number One, received a phone call. Brothers Two and Three were flying in for a quick visit to our frontier town in the rugged Far North and could we all meet at Brother Number Four's place for celebrating the reunion of the clan? The only other passenger on the tiny plane was the largest bottle of rum ever made at the Bundaberg Distillery.

The evening was inebriated but happy. I dispensed food, laughter and affection and, at midnight, I commenced my strategy for getting the husband home and bedded before the dawn.

We were finally mobile with myself doing the driving; another wifely duty found only in the fine print of The Contract. I congratulated myself on a successful getaway, naively relaxing as the cooling night breeze drifted through the broken window of our little utility. Then I made The Big Mistake!

'Look, honey! There's a huge carpet snake crossing the road. He's the biggest I've seen for a while around here.'

'Pull up! I want to look at him.'

'No, let's leave him be. He's probably going to visit his girlfriend in the scrub over there.' Even snakes might look forward to romantic Saturday evenings, I thought.

After the insistent demands of the husband, 'Stop the car! Pull over, pull over!', I acquiesced, but the person who instilled in me the virtues of being an obedient wife has much to explain.

To be fair, the husband is widely experienced in the handling of snakes, having dabbled in this domain since childhood. He does not behave foolishly even when alcoholically pickled and is very caring of the animal populace. The giant python was soon expertly loaded onto the ute. I did win one concession, in that The Beloved and The Reptile were to travel on the back, not in the cabin as initially suggested. No one chooses to vie with a cousin to the anaconda for possession of a utility's gear lever.

We pottered along towards our camp in the bush. All was fine until I chose to strike up a conversation.

'You all right, honey?' No answer.

'Honey, are you OK back there?' Silence.

Me, a tiny bit worried now: 'Don, answer me, please.'

'This [rude epithet] snake is trying to strangle me!'

Me, confident of husband's supreme reptile-handling ability, 'Oh, don't be silly. It's only a carpet snake.' Silence again.

'Don?' Worried enough now, I risk taking my eyes off the bush track and glance behind. Silence. 'Don!' very loudly.

'Aaargh!'

Never in real life have I heard anyone seriously choking, but all the horror films containing sinister strangulations have sounds just like this one.

I urged the little ute to lurch along the remaining stretch of track to our camp. This was a time for speed, not finesse. Stalled it, but dashed from cabin to tray in a twinkling.

Murder rose in my heart. The foolishness of anti-climax is apt to provoke this reaction, it seems. The Beloved slumbered, all innocence except for the vice-like grip of his hand on the snake. The Reptile had not enveloped The Spouse; The Spouse had enveloped The Reptile!

I flounced off — with some difficulty, as the track to our caravan home was uphill and over pure sand. But anger can lend dignity and menace to the lowliest action. Inside, I savagely pulled on my least sexy nightie, the lavender-with-white-flowers, neck-to-knee creation that I had bought for emergency trips to hospital, and viciously kicked the flimsy black lace number along the floor so that it slid into the far corner in a sulking heap. Romance was definitely off the menu for this little wifey on this particular evening in paradise.

Sleep also was as elusive as the winning numbers for my Saturday night Lotto ticket. The marital promises, 'From this day forward; In sickness and in health; For better, for worse', marched as if by teleprinter across my brain and back again, across my brain and back again.

I got out of bed intent on action. There they still were, seemingly glued to the tray of the utility. They resembled a pair of lovers ardently entwined, excepting that one was blissfully snoring, though not relinquishing his hold on his mate, while the other bore the saddest look of reptilian resignation I have ever seen.

Of spousely sympathy, I had none. My concerns were for the lady snake. I knew instinctively that this long-suffering reptile was female. What is more, she was a sweet-tempered female, or why did she not simply bite the fiend and be done with it?

She seemed to be weaving her upper body about, as if seeking something. I followed the pattern of the movements until I realised that she needed some type of stepping-stone between the level of the ute and the safety of the nearest scrub. Her strategy was now clear. She would lower her upper body to the stepping stone, grip it tightly and hang on doggedly until, hopefully, her captor lost interest in retaining her and released his hold.

I must provide the means to freedom.

There are no manuals on etiquette for this type of snaky dilemma, but I decided that an old iron kitchen chair would fit the bill nicely. I dashed back to camp, the slippery sand no longer a problem. The chair was placed just below the level of the ute. My sister snake launched her skinny shoulders into space and grasped the metal backing of the chair. The test of wills began with my barracking, 'You can do it, girl!'

The Spouse snuffled, squirmed and released his grip. I cheered in delight. Mrs Snake paused halfway down the leg of the chair, gave me what I could swear was a reptilian 'Thank you' look and then slithered gratefully away into the tropical night. My duty done by man and beast, I slept.

Hours later, a rum-smelling spouse bumbled his way into our caravan kingdom. The apparition aimed a sloppy kiss in my direction, patted me distractedly on the bottom and fell into the sleep of the innocent in a diagonal axis across the bed. I curled into the foetal position in the only tiny corner left for wives and began the religious chanting that would eventually lull me into blissful slumber: 'I promised for better or worse; I promised for better or worse ...'

No one chooses to vie with

a cousin to the anaconda for

possession of a utility's gear lever.

The Pride of Coochie Flats

THE WAIL TOOK US ALL by surprise. It rose up on the air like a thousand banshees. The windows shivered and Aunt Ethel's hideous vase ('It's a genuine heirloom, you ungrateful sod!') wobbled and teetered before settling firmly back on the mantle and grinning smugly at me.

'Strewth, Ruth!' I exclaimed, bouncing out of my chair. The *Coochie Flats Gazette* went flying, and as the pages rained down on me Em appeared in the doorway, her eyes as large as saucers. We were staring at each other like a pair of loons when off it went again. This time it sounded like someone had struck a pig with something particularly nasty.

Now, there's only one thing in Coochie Flats that makes a racket like that, and sure enough, there on the front lawn was our daughter Lizzy. A determined kind of girl is our Lizzy, never afraid to speak her mind, and she was sure speaking it now. Got it from her mother. So there she was, all five-foot nothing of her, and she was laying into her fiancé Josh something fierce. Her pretty little face was all screwed up and red, and the language! Didn't know the meaning of half of it, but I sure got the message. She was plenty mad! Spotting her ma, she collapsed with a final shriek and wept like her little heart was going to break. Em just gave me 'The Look' as she helped the prostrated Lizzy back to the house.

Now, thirty-odd years of marriage can teach a bloke a thing or two. One thing I've learned is 'The Look' is not good. It's trouble, big time. It means 'Joe Phillips, you do something about this, and I mean right now!'

So there you have it. That's why I'm standing here with this hulking great future son-in-law of mine and asking him why my girl saw fit to ring a peal over him just the day before the wedding, and won't I be needing my monkey suit after all? He just stood there like a mooning calf, which wasn't anything too out of the ordinary, then moved aside to expose the bent and crumpled bonnet of Viv the Valiant.

Now, some folks say I'm a bit slow. Myself, I like to think I'm just thorough, but even I could see at a glance that Viv the Valiant wasn't going anywhere for a while, and she certainly wouldn't be carrying the blushing bride to the church on the morrow. I scratched my chin and looked over to the house, where the sounds of caterwauling could still be heard coming from the front parlour. Now, Em's the expert on such matters. She should be after raising five daughters.

'There, there, love,' I could hear her say, 'Pa will sort it, you'll see.'

Well, what's a bloke to do? I hightailed it off to the shed like I had one of those banshees after me. Like I said, I'm no fool.

Ah, bliss. I grinned at Blue the cattle dog, and he grinned back at me, all teeth and lolloping tongue. 'Bloke's Heaven', we call this, home of the Beautest Yoot this side of the Wondalilly. There he was, as basic as dirt, but this baby could rumble! A lusty V8 heart that would give you chills; 165 kilowatts and torque as thick as concrete. And no poncy automatic either, like that milk crate on wheels Em had wanted. No, sir! Five on the floor with a 3.45:1 diff. The Beast works hard, plays hard, and when you lean on the throttle, makes every other drive you've ever had fade in comparison. So there we were, The Beast, Bluey and myself, all sitting grinning at each other, when I remembered what had sent me scuttling out here in the first place. Blue woofed sympathetically and laid a cold, wet nose on my slipper.

You know, from the very first time I ever beheld the blotchy red prune that was my little girl and she grabbed hold of my nose, I've been her slave, and I wasn't about to change now. If I had to carry her to the church on my back, so be it. And by crikey, if it didn't hit me in a blinding flash of white light! The greatest idea since Noah's missus told him to get the sheets off the line! Blue whined suspiciously and The Beast scowled.

'Now, boys,' I told them, 'we've all got sacrifices to make, and if I have to get all dolled up in that damn monkey suit, then you two can lend a hand as well!' Blue sneezed in disgust, but a man's gotta do what a man's gotta do.

I worked all night, washing and polishing The Beast till he shone. I put one of Em's nice chairs up on the tray and covered it with one of the 'good' bedspreads, then I set to work in the garden. Em's pride and joy, this flower garden, and by heaven there wasn't a bloom left to be seen by the time I had finished with it!

I met my red-eyed, sniffling princess at breakfast and led her out the front door. There was The Beast in all his glory! Transformed into a veritable bower of roses and daisies and goodness knows what else. Em gasped and dropped the teapot as she eyed the chicken wire arch dubiously. Not that any wire could be seen for the riot of blooms and fernery. Blue whimpered and hid his face, but Lizzy ... Lizzy, for once in her life, was speechless! Her blue eyes opened wide and her jaw fell. She couldn't believe what she was seeing!

Then the giggle started. It started somewhere in her belly, and rose like a tickle up through her throat, till she could stop it no longer and it burst forth. She threw her head back and laughed and laughed and laughed. Blue hung his head even lower.

'I'll ... be ... just ... like ... a ... fairy ... princess!' she gasped through her tears. 'Oh, Pa, thanks!'

And I got the biggest hug and kiss a proud dad could ever hope for. She looked again at the canopy of flowers and the 'throne' and collapsed in giggles once more. I don't know what Em quite meant when she said it was a good thing our girl was blessed with a sense of the ridiculous.

Anyway, they both did me proud that day. Even Blue condescended to ride along with Lizzy as Best Man. He said it was to keep The Beast company. I'll always remember the look on young Josh's face when his fairy princess arrived.

'Good on ya, love,' Em whispered to me, and squeezed my arm. She would have given me a big kiss, but the bunch of cherries on her hat kept slipping to one side if she moved too much. So, in the end, that's how the Pride of Coochie Flats made it to the church on time!

'Bloke's Heaven', we call this, home of the Beautest Yoot this side of the Wondalilly.

Buck's Night at the Bay

TWO OF MY MATES WERE getting married, and decided to have a combined buck's night. It was safety-in-numbers type of thinking. It didn't work, but that's another story.

A weekend up at Jurien Bay was organised.

Now, most of the guys that came were from the city, so they were straight into it. Yahooing as we drove through the Pinnacles. Riding on 'roo bars, bonnets, side rails, roofs. You name it, they hung off it.

With an afternoon of this under their belts you would have thought they'd be right to stay in the vehicles as we hit the dunes that night for some serious four-wheel driving.

This, however, was not the case, and while we were letting down our tyres Dames and Dunny (one of the bucks) were working out how they could ride on the back of my ute. This took a bit of thought, because it was a dual cab with a canopy. In the end they dropped the tailgate. They were going to stand on this and hold on to not a lot. Also, the other buck wasn't prepared to give up his front seat.

We set off, my vehicle in front, the other following closely behind.

We couldn't hear much from the cab, but those who remained up front were looking back and saw the groom-to-be, banging and screaming that he wanted to get off. He obviously had something to live for.

Dames, on the other hand, had already been married for twelve months, and he was going to keep on riding. While Dunny made his way off the tailgate, Dames managed to talk James, a friendly Indian dentist, into riding with him. Dames assured James that if they bent their knees they would be able to stay on while the tailgate bounced up and down beneath them. He was convinced. We took off again.

This time we had to gun it straight away to try and make it up a big dune which lay directly ahead of us.

We made it up the steep dune remarkably easily, and were still travelling at pace when we hit the top. My eyes opened wide and my heart hit my mouth. We were confronted with a landscape that was cratered like the surface of the moon. I hit the brakes, trying to slow down before we started on the dips. I knew we were going to get bounced around a fair bit in the cab, let alone what might happen to the tailgate.

We ended up going through three of these dips and ridges. Each of these was deeper than the one before it. We jerked to a stop in the sand. The other vehicle got to the top just in time to see it all happen. I didn't know what had happened to the tailgate riders, but I feared the worst. I jumped out of the cab, slamming the door on my way out.

Dames had been thrown off to one side. He had been face-planted into the dune and his foot was just centimetres from the back wheel. He was getting up by the time I got there. He was covered in sand and busy trying to spit some of it out of his mouth. If Dames was thrown this far, then where was James?

I was shouting out, 'James! James!' while looking out into the darkness. Now, James had a better tan than the rest of us, so I didn't think he would be too easy to find. I heard a quiet voice when I stopped shouting.

'David! David!' Where was he?

He was on the roof. Up the front of the cab, and he had knocked my aerials over on the way there!

'Are you OK?' I asked with great concern, not knowing what sort of condition he was going to be in.

All he said was 'David, David, I'm all right, but could you please open your door?'

'What? Why's that, James?' I couldn't figure him out.

'Because my fingers are stuck in there,' he said.

He hadn't suffered any injuries until I slammed his fingers in the door of the dual cab ute!

A Few Cones in the Back of a Ute

THIS ONE WILL DEFINITELY MAKE the pot-heads sit up and think seriously about joining the army.

It's about February '93, I'm the section commander of 2 Section, 7 Platoon, Charlie Company, the First Battalion RAR. Together with my men, I'm running a VCP (vehicle check point) about 40 kilometres east of Baidoa, in Somalia. We've been sitting there checking vehicles using the MSR (main supply route) for a couple of days now, and if you have ever done this sort of work you'll know it can get pretty tedious to say the least.

Anyway, along comes this old Landcruiser ute — it doesn't look much different from any of the other vehicles that we've searched, except from about 100 metres out you could see that the occupants had a pretty worried look about them. Naturally anything like that tends to put one on the lookout for trouble, and by the looks of these guys something was definitely going on.

Now, due to all our previous contacts having been with young blokes between eighteen and thirty-five years old, as these clowns were as well, we were really suspicious. Approximately ten seconds pass, these guys pull up and the search begins. First we get them to switch off the vehicle. They pretend not to understand. A rifle point's at the driver's head and he suddenly speaks Oxford English. Next we unload the passengers and driver, and they are all taken to the side of the road and searched for any concealed goodies.

Nothing, not a single thing is found. So we turn our attention to the vehicle, and with the aid of the driver we start at the front: bonnet up, and searched, nothing; cabin doors opened, cabin searched, still naught.

Now, this guy can see we are getting pretty pissed off and he starts to giggle. I turn around and his mates are off to the side of the road and they're in hysterics. Now I'm startin' to think these characters are having a lend of us, when suddenly the whole Section is hit by this smell.

For about ten seconds we sit there staring at each other in disbelief, then one of my blokes starts to laugh and dives into the back tray. He proceeds to throw these big potato sacks over the side. The rest of the search team make short work of these sacks.

Inside are over 250 parcels a bit bigger than a coke can, and each is chockers full of compressed heads of marijuana! Now, we are in an Active Service Zone, and I'm buggered if they mentioned anything about what we should do if we come across a ute full of cannabis. So I'm on the radio to a higher authority. 'Let them and their property go,' they say. So after consoling my men, who are near to tears, I send them on their way.

Now, these geezers think we are the tops for allowing them to keep their pot, and as a goodwill gesture offer to sell us a couple of parcels, which were about four ounces each, at $2.00 a shot. Needless to say we, being good Aussie soldiers representing our beloved nation and all, refused their generosity. (Bad luck pot-heads!)

A few days later we were tasked with more pressing matters, and whilst being briefed I was informed that marijuana was now illegal in Somalia and any found was to be confiscated and handed in to be destroyed. By burning no doubt!

Now I'm startin' to think these characters are having a lend of us, when suddenly the whole Section is hit by this smell.

Johnny's Beaut Ute

IT WAS FUNNY THE DAY I saw my husband's pathetic figure climb out of the car as he unloaded the old, battered ute that was sitting on the trailer. He was looking pretty grotty and his hair was tousled after that big hunt.

I stood in the driveway trying to stifle a giggle. 'What are you gunna do with that rusty-looking thing? We've got enough rubbish around here,' I remarked. John looked at me as if I had done him a grave injustice. 'Just wait and see, dear ... I bet she'll turn out like you wouldn't believe,' John replied, narrowing his eyes with an air of unmistakable optimism.

He was fair dinkum about it. He was being ambitious, I thought. I was quite sceptical at the prospect. I found it hard to believe then that a dud-looking machine like that ute could ever be restored to its original beauty.

John worked as a boilermaker and had an extraordinary love for engines, his boss had once said. Motor-mad person, I reckon. He had this great big shed jam-packed with his collection of car parts, some of which he fished out from the tip. Young chaps building an old bomb knew where to go when hunting for some parts. 'Go and see Johnny' was the word of mouth.

John battled with the ute for a week after he towed it home. He knew it would involve a helluva lot of hard yakka, hundreds of cuppas (to keep him awake while restoring it) and heaps of engineering smarts. He was obsessed with the ute. His aim was to create a Euro sports ute. Piece by piece he laboriously flicked all the parts apart except for the body. Everything had been smoothed out, and all baddies changed into goodies, and the six-spotter converted into a V8 predator. A real predator, 'cause it could roar all right! I was not that well-versed in car parts; I only knew a bit about it because I had often heard my husband yakking about his endless tales to his mates. I had gotten sick of listening to his 'yoot yarns' after a while, you see.

Our shed was always neck-deep in creepy-looking fellas checking out John's ute. Blokes of all sorts, heavily tattooed, pierced and long-haired, who would greet me, 'How are yer doin'?' if they happened to see me. They would open the bonnet up and shove their heads under it, examining the engine as though they had never seen one before. A good peek under the ute like they thought they knew what they were looking at.

John's projects really cheesed me off, since he spent many a late night in the shed. I consider my husband a real work addict — which means that he plunges himself into work like someone hurling himself off a hangar.

One night I rushed into the shed, since he wouldn't come in to have his tea after I'd called him a dozen times. 'You could've married that clunker instead of me,' I hissed as I put my hands on my waist.

My annoyance suddenly changed into laughter as I saw that white-faced John had black marks all over his face and a generous smudge of grease on it too. Still, he managed to say his all-too-familiar line: 'You know I love you, dear, I wouldn't have married you if I didn't love you.' He wiped his greasy hands, sat me down on the chair and gave me a gentle kiss. End of blue.

We had a bit of a disagreement about the colour. 'I'd like to see that ute hot pink,' I suggested, imagining the pretty colour from what I'd seen in a car magazine.

'Hmmm … pink is a bit common, I reckon. I'll paint it black and blue,' he said, as he ambled off to test the engine.

John revved the engine so hard that it produced a thundering loud noise, which startled the little old lady next door who was having her afternoon nap at the time. The noise sent her out of the house whingeing and her dog charged out behind her. She looked mortified as she sticky-beaked over the fence and sounded peppery. 'I shan't put up with that, that cranky old John shouldn't be allowed to go revving that noisy motor at this time of the day. He'd be better doing that out in the paddock instead. I'll be forced to notify the police if he does it again. Mark my word.' Then she stomped inside.

I sort of agreed with her, really. I was only young then but I could not stand the deafening noise pollution either. I felt as though the ground quaked whenever John did that revving, not to mention the terrible black smoke it produced.

After twelve months John's mission was finally over. The yucky yoot grew into a real beauty. The motor was a GT 351. The body work was splashed with black and blue paint, with striking yellow fire stickers slanted across the body, the inscription 'Falcon' obliquely stuck in the middle part and a personalised plate that read 'Johnny'. Quite impressive.

But there was this lumpy contraption protruding on top of the bonnet. I asked my hubby what it was.

'It's a scoop, woman!' he said ingratiatingly.

'And what does it do there?' I queried.

'It covers two carburettors.'

Needless to say, we were wrapt with the finished product. That was John's first serious build-up, and he received quite a lot of praise, which made him put on his big watermelon smile. Now and again he would take the rocket for a test drive, but never when the weather looked iffy.

He decided to enter the ute in a South Australia 'Show 'n' Shine' car show. I had even grown to like John's ute, 'cos it was immaculate, cool and dazzling — not something I'd drive to go shopping, though. He paid 500 smackers for the gawky refuse that had metamorphosed into one fine-looking machine.

One day an American friend visited us, and after we had had our dinner John said to the Yankee: 'C'mon into the shed and have a look at my ute.'

'Ute? What's a ute?' He looked at John as though waiting for him to explain the never-heard word.

So John said, 'Utility car, ute for short.'

Then he said, 'Ow, that's right, a pickup or a truck!'

The day of the car show had finally arrived. I smiled smugly that morning as John left for the show. I gazed at the used-to-be-an-eyesore package, its paint shining brilliantly in the morning sun. Even John seemed to sparkle, looking nicely scrubbed in his crisp white shirt. He cuddled me ta-ta and then hit the road towing his pride and joy.

The yucky yoot grew into

a real beauty.

Just One of the Boys

THE CLASS OF '79 SCHOOL reunion was that night. We still knew most of them. After all, even if we didn't exactly see them every day, we'd see them every week or so when they came into town for groceries, rat bait, cattle wormers or economy-sized sacks of dog tucker. A two-pub town: if you didn't stop in at the top pub, you'd be at the bottom one. The old blokes usually took the bottom one 'cause they let your dog in, long as it'd stay under your chair and behave itself.

You could pick the locals at a glance. Working men in working men's elastic-sided boots, a bit down at heel and coated in cow shit and mud. But even before you had a chance to see their boots, you could pick them when they drove up. If their ute wasn't a Holden, it was a Ford. Only the hobby farmers and wives drove sedans or station wagons.

So, when the boys and me were sculling the compulsory New or Old and pondering the relative merits of pour-on over dipping, we knew, without thinking, that the bloke parking the BMW behind the wired-on tailgate of Pete Foster's rusty HK was a city boy. Even before we caught a waft of chilled air from the air conditioning and he locked the doors with one of those remote control thingees. You could have run a solar generator off the polish on his hood, used it to power a neon sign with the message 'Urban Professional' and stuck it on his back with duct tape. He couldn't have been more conspicuous. Like a snowdrift in a sheep-dagging yard.

But there was something familiar about him. I just couldn't put me finger on it.

He nodded to us on the way in, his shirt disturbingly white and crisp, trousers pressed, gold watch gleaming. Pete half turned his head in that slow way Pete's always had, then commented as he went back to leaning on the rail, staring blankly at the familiar main street, 'Gees. The things ya see when ya ain't got a gun.'

It was my round. Ellen had them half pulled before I got to the bar. 'How's Suzie?' she asked as I slapped a twenty down on the slop towel.

'Better. The little bugger's a good looker, like his dad. Might even keep him.'

Mr White-and-Wrinkle-free twisted in his seat to face us. 'Congratulations.'

'What fer?'

'On your son?'

'What the hell d'ya mean?' Was this some lawyer bloke on a mission to prove the paternity of some city kid?

'You just said . . . you know, about your wife . . .'

'Either you drink a shitload faster than me, mate, or yer hearin' things.' Then the dead koala dropped. 'Suzie's me dog, mate. Just littered.'

'Oh.'

'Yeah, six pups and lost all but one, and he was about as pretty as road kill fer a while. She was crook, but she's OK now.'

'I see. Kevin McKay,' he introduced himself.

A second deceased marsupial descended. I knew this bloke.

'Class of '79?'

'Same.'

'Well, just give us a sec while I get rid of these, and I'll buy you a beer.' I delivered the boys their schooners. 'What took ya so long? Could've died of bloody dehydration.'

'Kevin McKay. Bloke in the Beamer.'

'Not Kev from school?'

'Yeah.'

He decided to come with me. If you were looking for two blokes more different, you couldn't have gone past Pete and Kev. Pete, if you could get him to talk at all, kept it short and simple, and only did it when absolutely necessary. Put a beer in his hand, and the only way you'd know he was breathing was because he'd bend the elbow from time to time.

Kevin was all shiny exterior, movement and noise. He threw his arms about like a blue heeler at a cat show and, within thirty seconds of hitting the bar stool beside us, he was bragging about his big city business, his collection of sports cars, his model wife and two football hero sons. Pete raised his head once during Kev's marathon bull-shitting bout to glance over the bar. Maybe he was looking for something big enough to block up the hole in Kev's face.

We left early and headed for the reunion. Pete always left the pub a half hour before dark 'cause his headlights had died in '82 and he'd never got around to fixing them. Buggered if I knew how he'd get the old girl through rego when his dad retired and sold the garage/general store/truck stop. He had parts in there that you couldn't get from a collector, and could pull a gearbox faster than any three other blokes.

I took the Esky out of the front seat before I picked Pete up. There were two advantages in this. First, if Pete came with me, he wouldn't have to drive home in his beast with his Dolphin torch on the dash. Second, if

I was driving, Pete could make an attempt at breaking the tinnie record set at the last reunion back in '94. I didn't want him to get a head start, so I stuck the Esky in the shed.

I'd forgotten about Kev. The Beamer had pulled in just behind us, a bit dustier now but still as glaringly conspicuous as tits on a bull. Without a conspiring word, Pete and I were out of the ute and away before Kev had a chance to talk to us. By the time he got inside, we were buried as far away from the door as humanly possible without going through the rear wall and falling the ten feet into the paddock out back. Two minutes later you could hear his voice, despite the crowd, giving the same speech he'd practised on us in the pub.

Pete stood, contemplatively, for a few seconds before he spoke. 'Did ya leave yer toolbox in?'

'Ya had yer feet on it the whole way in, yer stupid bastard. Why?'

'I think I'm going to have to wire his gob shut.'

By eleven o'clock there wasn't a soul in the class of '79 who hadn't heard that speech, but most of them were too written off to care. Pete was within three tinnies of breaking the record, and was still upright. I knew that he had at least four more cans in him once he went in the legs, so I thought the new record was pretty securely in hand. The noise level had risen as the keg levels had fallen, so at least we couldn't hear Kev any more.

That was when Sergeant Bob arrived. I didn't think much of it at first, 'cause we'd invited him along for a few drinks when we'd spotted him sticking fines on tourists' cars for parking infringements a few days back. Even though he was class of '77 we knew he was keen on Ellen, the only single girl over thirty in town, and we felt it was our duty to get them together.

But Rob was in uniform. When he strolled over to Kev, the conversation died like a bug on a windscreen.

'Kevin McKay?'

'Err . . . yeah.'

'We just got a call down at the station. You have a son, Gregory Alan McKay? Aged 18, unemployed, living at your rented address in Dubbo?'

'Ummm . . . yeah.' Dubbo?

'Unfortunately, he's just wrapped a utility, rego CUR 020, around a tree in the front yard of a residence in High Street.'

'Me ute!'

'He's uninjured, but it seems that he was running from police at the time.'

'Why? He's got a licence.'

'Actually, he doesn't. He lost it after that culpable driving incident earlier this year.'

'What incident?'

'When he stole a car to visit his mother in gaol. You'd better come with me. We'll drive over, but this could take some time.'

'But I have to return the car! It'll cost me a week's wages at the meatworks if I don't get it back before ten o'clock tomorrow.'

We drove the car back for him. It was the least we could do for an old mate. I couldn't hardly blame Suzie when she puked all over the velour upholstery in the back. After all, she'd never been in a sedan. She was a ute dog.

Ute Surfin'

SOME OF US GOT 'EM and some of us ain't. Me, I've got 'em — fleas, that is; but then, so do most dogs. Not to worry ... kinda sorts us streetwise mongrels from them prissy, pedigree couch potatoes.

For me, with my shaggy, brittle fur, every day is a bad hair day. And for a touch of feral contrast there's a patch of mange on my rump — a bit like a mohawk. But I still have a thick head of brindle hair — which is more than I can say for my boss, Bluey. And just 'cause ya can't see my peepers, doesn't mean I have a problem with my eyesight. From in here it's a bit like lookin' through a slim-line, tan and grey, vertical blind — custom-made sunnies, ya might say.

Smell! ... What smell? That's honest sweat, I'll have ya know. I'm a workin' dog. No, I don't mean one of them intellectual types like yer kelpies or border collies who lecture to a bunch of sheep for a livin', or that poser Kane, TV's hunky stunt pin-up. And ya wouldn't catch me struttin' me stuff on the big screen either, not with them egotistical tree-sniffers Lassie and Beethoven in the business. In my opinion, Benji's the only one's got any real talent in that snooty crowd. Did ya know they spend at least half their day in one of them poochy parlours? Bloody K9 torture, that is!

You try keepin' yer coat glossy and manageable when yer ridin' shotgun in the back of a rustin' ute with a concrete mixer and a dag-encrusted load of scaffoldin' for company. Ya see, I'm a brickie's labourer.

Me and Bluey, we were doin' this job out the back of Woop Woop ... wanted to get it finished before dark

... save us comin' all the way back for an hour's work the next day. Got it all done, too — just don't look too closely at the top three courses ... gets a bit skew-whiff when he's pushed for time, the ol' Blue.

It was a Friday afternoon, middle of winter, and damn cold in the back of the old ute, too, let me tell ya. As we wound our way down the narrow mountain road, Bluey turned on the headlights, although at that eerie time of dusk they never do much to light the way.

There's me in the back, legs splayed, expertly shiftin' my weight as I surf my way through each new curve. But with the promise of a coldie in his nostrils, Bluey couldn't resist nudgin' the accelerator out of each turn.

Mind you, he's a good driver, but I wish he'd try, just once, ridin' in the back when he's doin' his Dick Johnson impersonation. The rear end started to swing wider. I could hear the tie-down ropes strainin' against the concrete mixer as it jolted and lurched with each whiplash.

'Struth, Blue, are you deaf?' I barked frantically. 'The mixer's chuckin' an atomic wobbly back here!'

The rear tyres were skiddin' into the gravel shoulders and I realised there was no way Bluey could see me through the clouds of dust the ute was spewin' up. I could feel my cement-crudded paws losin' their grip. Now, for those of you who aren't familiar with ute-surfin', let me explain. Once ya lose the plot, yer a goner — that is, until ya hit another straight, then ya can usually snatch the chance to plant yerself on all fours again.

So there I was, bein' hurled from side to side, not to mention coppin' a clobberin' from the floats and trowels that were flyin' across the open cab. I panicked when I saw the spirit level cart-wheelin' towards me and tucked my tail in for protection. Just as well — damn thing nearly jabbed me in the jollies!

'Eh, Blue, steady on, mate! The beer'll still be cold when we get to the local.' I skidded on the plumb-bob and went crashin' against the gyratin' mixer. The boss obviously hadn't heard me over Martin/Molloy blarin' on the radio. I barked louder, addin' a few familiar adjectives sure to grab his attention.

I woke up in complete darkness at the bottom of a gully to the creepy sound of the nocturnal locals scavengin' for a feed in the scrub. I just lay there with a terrible pain in my left hip and thought of Bluey … probably settled in at the pub, guzzlin' down his third schooner.

By dawn my mangy leg was swollen to more than twice its normal size, and I'd lost count of how many times I'd heard the familiar rumble of the ute cruisin' past. There it was again. It was slowin' down. Shh … wait for it, wait for it … yep, there she goes, that familiar crunch of the mixer as the ute comes to a stop. I'd know that sweet sound anywhere.

I barked — or was it a yelp? No, I'm no sook — it was definitely a bark.

'Hey Bluey, down here mate!'

Four weeks later and I'm back to ute surfin' again, only now I'm shackled in my flashy new harness. This *is* great — no more wipeouts! And ya should see the fancy tricks this gizmo lets me do. Abseilin' off the mixer, hangin' ten from the gunnels an' bungy jumpin' off the roof. Reckon I should ask Bluey for a helmet and shin pads, then you'd really see some action!

Big Spenders

I'VE STILL GOT THE FJ ute that we got married in twenty-six years ago this December.

What a knees-up the wedding was! We decided to give everyone a real treat and have the do on a ferry on Sydney Harbour. We hired the 'Prolong', which was the ferry that sank in the harbour a few years later, but thankfully we stayed afloat. Me mate and I filled the ute up with three 18-gallon kegs and a nine-gallon so that the guests wouldn't get thirsty during the four hours on the boat on a hot December arvo.

My wife came in a hire car, but I didn't see much of that because we were still getting the grog started without a regulator on the beer plant.

It was a good turn-out. My uncle fell down the stairs head-first; the ladies got photos taken with their dresses blowing up; my dad and my uncles all had squinty eyes. When we pulled up to the wharf next to where the Water Police were then, we thought they were going to arrest us all.

So me and me new missus got into the ute with all the ribbons and tin cans and drove off under the Harbour Bridge heading for the North Coast. Well, I was so buggered that we could only make the motel at Mt Colah about 20 miles out of Sydney (miles, because that's what the ute's speedo reads).

The next night we made it to Scotts Head, some 350 miles north, and we pitched a tent that my best man lent me. By the time we got to Coffs Harbour the next day I'd had it with driving, and since I only had a week off and the wedding took up one day, we didn't have much time left. I'd put a rack on the top of the ute the week before so that I could go surf skiing, and it worked real fine.

We stayed in a motel on the corner into Coffs, where someone was killed during its construction.

On the way back we sort of ran out of time and couldn't decide where to stay, so we pulled up under the railway bridge at Wyong, moved a bit of gear around in the back of the ute and slept in there. The only trouble with that was that my wife didn't wear shoes and socks to bed and her feet got bitten by mozzies.

We are pretty sure that the ute had something to do with our daughter Claire, because she was born nine months later.

To celebrate the good service the old girl's given me I have done her up. So far when I divide the cost by the number of years I've had her, it works out at about $450 a year. Because it's our twenty-sixth anniversary this year I plan to take both girls away again. We plan to do the same trip in December 2001. But it will be four-star all the way and maybe for more than six days.

So if you see my brown FJ ute heading up the North Coast in December 2001, say hello. You will know it; it'll have my surfboard on the top. See ya.

If you see my brown FJ ute heading

up the North Coast, say hello.

You will know it; it'll have my

surfboard on the top.

The True Story of My Mongrel Ute

BEING AN OLD COCKY I can't remember the number of utes I've had, but one old girl does stick in my mind. And I'll bet the previous owners would remember her too — well, those who haven't long gone to God. She'd done more than a good lifetime's service well before I bought her for an old runabout on the farm.

Christies Motor Auctions in Melbourne will give you an idea of the era we're talking about here. The old HD had probably been passed in half a dozen times before I got to buy her on that sale day; can't remember what I paid for the old dear, but I had no illusions she hadn't been pretty well worked over by her former owners.

From the rego papers I found she had last been owned by some other cocky from Echuca, but heaven only knows how many other owners had had their hands on her before that. But the engine ran, the exterior was passable and the Hydromatic two-speed auto box seemed OK. The floor was a bit rusted out, but she'd see out another year or two on my farm up the Mallee. A mate of mine in Abbotsford could doctor her up enough to get an RWC off an easygoing mechanic in Hoddle Street. With the paperwork completed, I drove her up the bush.

Within a month on the farm, part of her old, rusted arse dropped out, leaving a gaping hole in the floor behind the seat. This allowed clouds of dust to fumigate the cabin in summer, and in the wet weather you'd be driving through a puddle, and a sauna of clouds of steam would pour off the hot muffler. The obvious answer to these problems? Always drive with the windows down! Subsequently, she got so grotty inside you could hardly see the St Christopher's medal that someone had glued to the dash.

Nevertheless, I was prepared to tolerate the old girl. But like most old girls, she developed a nasty habit. When feeding out a few bales in the paddock the Hydromatic would sometimes gently drop back into gear and start backing quietly across the paddock. However, she wasn't hard to catch, and having lived with a few cantankerous girls in my life, I was prepared to tolerate this little idiosyncrasy.

Probably a bad habit, but I quite often left her idling, the reason being she was a bit hard to restart when she was hot. Besides, the battery was not all that flash either. 'Bloody automatics! I could get years out of stuffed batteries by parking manuals on the damn wall and roll-starting them,' I'd bemoan.

'Like women, if they let you down once they'll let you down again,' said a mate of mine, who'd had had more floozies than good feeds. And I should have heeded his philandering philosophies. As most ute drivers know, there is an obscure but definite relationship between utes and feminine behaviour. And this old HD had been the darling of many a man in her day.

I was doing a bit of scabbing down the tip one day, after I had dumped the Bathurst burr I had chipped out from the boundary paddock. I grovelled about over the edge of the steep cutting, picking up the loaves of stale bread the town baker had chucked out. Well, the chooks and pigs enjoyed a change in diet, didn't they?

The old HD was idling about 20 metres away where I had left it. You guessed it! A gentle click and she started rolling back towards the steep edge of the tip. Her plan to suicide was one thing, but I was frightened by her desire to take me with her. She was heading straight towards me at head height.

A retreat down the wall of the tip was no choice; it was a jungle of all types of crap down there. Dropping my armful of reclaimed bread, I tried to escape uphill, but in my panic I couldn't gain traction up the slope of knee-deep papers, empty paint tins and other garbage. Everything slowed down, like in a dream when you're being chased.

I stood riveted. God! This could be the end! Buried in garbage under the rusting bowels of the old HD was an undignified way to end it all. And a weird thought flashed by me: my demise would add a little colour to the limited excitement that happens in this town.

She was bearing down on me. I was getting life's instant replay before my eyes. I'd heard this happens when you're about to cash it in. I was a goner! I now stood petrified as she slowly but relentlessly backed towards me.

Luckily, that dusty Mick medal glued on the dash must have been still active. Miraculously, a quarter house-brick caught the driving side front wheel, slewed it and spun the steering. I got a good view of the greasy front end as she swung away and passed at eye level. I'd had a reprieve.

Regaining my faculties, I got down on all fours and crawled up the side. However, now there was no urgency, she had taken up a circular orbit on the filled and levelled section of the tip reserve. The perfidious old tart now backed around innocently in tight circles awaiting my attention. Although still a little fazed, I opened the door as she passed and clambered inside. I drove down the street and bought a new battery.

Nevertheless, the treacherous old girl still gave a bit more service after the tip incident, but I never again trusted her to sit waiting for me on idle. I eventually replaced her. She was retired to the old hay shed, where she sat sulking for a couple of years until a neighbour offered me a hundred bucks for her for parts. I just had to let her go.

As my mate said, 'If they let you down once, they'll let you down again.'

He's My Ute and I'll Keep it That Way!

YOU SEE, MY STORY GOES like this. Since I was a tiny kid I always wanted a 4WD ute so I could go bush-bashing and take my horse wherever I wanted to go . . . and let's not forget my trusty dog Kip.

The teen years soon came and then I hit eighteen. I was nineteen when Dad found me my first wheels. I named the car Bess, 'cause she was a faithful old thing. She was a Holden Gemini. Many a B&S she did see. Back windows you could barely see out of due to those beloved B&S stickers. They called me 'Meals on Wheels', 'cause we did many a mile, Bess and me, driving, eating and sleeping. She took me to Cooma, to the land of the High Country where the brumbies roam. There is a song that goes something like this:

I got my 4WD and I'm ready to roll,

I wanna go flying up an old dirt road,

Up in the hills where the brumbies roam,

This land must surely be God's own.

Not being mean to Bess, but my heart was still set on one of those 4WD utes. A Hilux, in fact. I knew one day I would be flying up and down those roads in one. Poor old Bess, she died after a year up there. 'This is it,' I thought. 'Now I can buy my dream ute.'

I made many suggestions to my dad. Example: 'Hilux, hey Dad, they are a good ute. Falcon or Subaru perhaps?' Dad would pace around, scratch behind his ear. 'No, it's gotta be a diesel,' he would say. 'We have always had diesel utes and they go forever. Also, the way you drive, girl, you need something with guts.'

All his daughter wanted was a ute. Not just any plain ute, but a ute that stood out from the rest. A Hilux ute, with big, fat tyres, a rollbar, sidesteps. And let's not forget the bullbar to knock over anything or anybody that comes near us. Colour didn't matter, as long as a good scrub would make it look sparkling clean after a hard day in the bush. And he had to have GUTS, be macho and stand proud amongst other utes.

Once again, Dad came through with the goods. 'I found ya ute,' he said one day.

It had four doors, not two. It was sort of a ute. 'What's it like?' I said.

'Well it's a Nissan 2WD, dual cab with a lockable canopy. Yes, let's not forget it's a diesel. Cheap, too, at $5500,' he said.

'What colour?' I asked.

'Yellow.'

'Bullbar?'

'Yes.'

Oh well, I thought, nobody will lose me. He means well, my dad, but I just couldn't help thinking about my dream ute. Reluctantly I toddled off from Cooma to pick up the ute.

Well, it wasn't love at first sight. 'Gee, it's long,' I said to Dad. Yes, and very bright yellow, too. Bullbar — well yes, a tiny one. No fat tyres, rollbar or sidesteps. It took us two a little while to get to know each other, then I got to like the old girl. The tray, having a lockable canopy, was very handy for carrying stuff in, particularly bags of horse feed. It was supposed to be for the dog too. She would hear the rattle of the keys and fly straight into the passenger seat in front. She would nod and bark at the passing traffic, and duck her head when we drove under bridges. She was a black and tan kelpie. Had a keen eye for sheep, too, when I got the chance to take her.

We did many a mile, that ute, dog and I, towing the old horse float around, too. I nicknamed her Gutsy, 'cause when we ventured back to the land of the rolling green hills (South Gippsland) she towed that horse float like it was an empty trailer.

Well, that ute had had a tough life, and once again I had a ute that was on her last legs. Well, with money in the bank and a small loan from them, too, I decided it was time to buy myself a REAL ute.

I looked around for months in the 4WD magazines and the *Trading Post*, but had no luck. Then with help from a friend, I finally found HIM!

Picture this: a sparkling white Hilux 4WD, two-door — not four — lift kit, long tray, rollbar, bullbar, sidesteps, towbar, black tarpaulin, tinted windows AND a CD player!

It was love at first sight. My dream ute was here! He had power, guts and he stood out from the crowd. And to top it off, he had these black and grey stickers above his rear tyres — the finishing touch, I thought to myself.

In my eyes he was HOT. The man in my life, for sure. Took him for a test drive. That was it. My heart was as good as gone. It was the proudest day of my life handing that cheque over. Now, a name, I thought. Brain ticking. That's it! BJ! That's what I'll call him!

I've had him now for twelve months or more. Many a good time had in that ute, for sure. Been christened, too, if ya know what I mean!

I travel on my own now, as my beloved dog has passed on. Tried to tackle a moving tyre, but the tyre got to her first. BJ has taken me on another adventure up to North Queensland to work on a cattle station. Many a story to tell later, I'm sure. So here's cheers to all you ute-lovers out there.

And you small kids who dream of owning your dream ute, don't give up, 'cause dreams eventually become reality.

Finally, there's a tribute song I have for BJ but I've changed the words. Instead of 'She's my Ute and I'll keep it that way' it's:

He's my ute and I'll keep it that way

BJ's my ute and he's here to *stay*!

It was love at first sight.

My dream ute was here!

Thank Heavens for Utes!

I WAS RIDING MY PUSHIE home from school one day when I had a stack which broke my shoulder. To my surprise I was entitled to compo, so that was a bonus. Unfortunately, I still had to go to school. Bugger!

I was in the market for a paddock-basher to hoon around the property and practise my driving, as I was almost old enough to get my licence. The only requirements were that it could go, was a manual and was a ute (of course).

I was scouting the local *Trading Post* and my eyes lit up when it jumped from the page. A 1973 XA Ford Falcon ute for $400. I was on the blower quick-smart and sure enough, it was still there. My old man and I rocked up the next night in pitch black and all we had was a crappy torch. It turned out that the guy's missus had caught him driving the unregistered ute one night when he was pissed as a fart, so it was either him or the ute that went. The ute was rough, all right, and certainly not worth the price tag even if it was a ute, so I offered him $250. BUT, he said if it was out of his sight by the end of the week I could have it for $200. (I think he was feeling a little backed up.)

I handed over the cash and she was mine. Next day the towie dropped her to my place and she really was all mine. Now was time for the fun to begin, along with the discovery of rust, and lots of it. Driving her with a broken shoulder was going to be a challenge, but that wasn't going to stop me.

Later on I had to go to the doc for a check-up to keep the injury comp people happy, and it was suggested that I needed to do exercises using my shoulder, like stirring movements, up and down and so on. As the beast was column shift and drove like a tank, she was perfect for my exercises, so off I went with my mates to do some circle work.

We had this pumpkin patch that was overgrown with weeds, like 6 or 7 feet tall. We'd go flying through it, with no visibility, and at the end of the day all that there was for tea was mashed pumpkin!

By that time the column shift had shat itself, so I cut a hole in the floor and, with a dog leash, I would pull the linkages up into gear. Sometimes it wouldn't work, so you'd have to hop out and change gear. That was interesting.

One night after a school function, me mates and I came home to take the beast for a spin. I'd managed to find a back seat from one of those luxury Jap cars for $5 at the markets, which was great for riding in the back. Anyway, with one headlight we were off fangin' around the bush trying to spot each other. Somehow we managed not to kill ourselves. Eventually it became light and, as we were all rooted, we admired our handiwork on the grass and drove to school, which is where we got to catch up on some sleep.

She was a great old ute. She taught many people how to drive, including my ten-year-old sister.

And now, when I look out the back shed and see her on blocks with a smile on her dial, I know the beast retired happy and well worn-out. Rest in peace, beast.

She was a great old ute. She taught many people how to drive, including my ten-year-old sister.

The 1924 Dodge

PERHAPS IT WAS WHEN the era changed, but the conversion of John's Dodge to a utility happened when he was away in the islands fighting for the country. Lorna had to stay home and manage the farm as well as feed and clothe five children, four strapping boys and one precocious tomboy girl. Eunice was the second eldest of the five. It was Eunice's idea to convert John's 1924 Dodge.

Eunice and her eldest brother Raymond were always in charge of the other kids. Raymond was seventeen and his sister sixteen. Ray wanted to go and fight the hated Japs who had killed his Uncle Dave in New Guinea. Lorna wouldn't let him go. She needed a strong man around the farm to drive the tractor, put in the crops, and to cut the hay in the spring. He was a big lad, almost a man, but not quite.

Eunice was sick of loading up two or three bales of hay at a time and taking the gig out to the paddock to feed the cows and then coming back and doing it all again. It took up too much of her day. Their father's 1924 Dodge was still sitting in the shed, and they knew that Lorna only used it to go to town occasionally for groceries and the mail. Everything else they needed they provided for themselves from the farm, selling their grain crop to help feed the people in the cities and the men overseas fighting.

'Ray, let's take the back seat out of the car and put a platform there and turn it into a small truck,' she said to him one day.

'Dad will kill us,' said Raymond.

'No he won't, we can put it back together before he comes home,' said Eunice, 'whenever that may be.'

'What's the plan?' asked Raymond.

'Well, I can remove the seats and stuff by undoing those bolts,' said Eunice. 'You can use that leftover timber near the machinery shed for the tray. It will be great! We can take ten bales of hay or more at once out to the paddocks for the cattle. Not only that, but if we have to go fencing we can take more wire and tools with us than what we can get in the gig. This is such a good idea!'

Eunice was absolutely chuffed with her idea. They set about working in the shed with the doors closed. It only took a day and their new small truck was ready.

'What can we call it?' Eunice asked Raymond, when they had finished and were admiring their handiwork.

'What about calling it a utility?' said Raymond. 'After all, it is going to be utilised for everything from now on.'

He grimaced at the untidiness of their handiwork. The planks hung well out over the back of the car that was now a ute. From the front it looked normal. However, the rear view looked like a cyclone had flattened a cubby house on top of the rear of the car. But it looked like Eunice's idea would work.

The next day they decided to test out the ute, and loaded it up with hay bales. The hastily made tray squeaked and groaned under the load, but miraculously it all stayed together. Raymond drove and they set off to feed the cows. At each bump the tray sounded like it was falling apart, but it didn't. Raymond drove very slowly, while Eunice climbed up on top and fed out the hay.

'This is perfect,' she called down to Raymond from on top of the load of hay.

For several months they continued to use the ute for their work around the farm. After her initial surprise, Lorna agreed the vehicle was now much more functional about the place. In the back of her mind she wondered what her John would say when he saw his beloved 1924 Dodge cannibalised in this manner.

One day, a Sunday, Lorna was sick in bed. The children had the run of the place. Eunice decided for all of them that it was a great day for a Sunday drive. Raymond disagreed. It was OK to drive around the farm, he argued, but out on the roads was a different matter. Eunice and the other kids wore down his resolve. Their excitement was infectious and he succumbed to the sibling pressure. Off they went in a cloud of dust.

Out on the road to town they encountered the neighbours in their shiny Packard. It was jet-black, with white trimming on the tyres. They had their canopy down and the mother and daughters had their sunbonnets on, tied under their chins. The Reverend was driving them around.

Ray cruised up alongside. The rest of them made faces. The Reverend tried to speed up, Raymond matched him, and before long, after Raymond was egged on by his brothers and sister, there was a drag underway. Raymond was gunning the Dodge, and the Reverend Thomas was also trying to speed past them. Mrs Ridgeway was telling the reverend to go faster. The three younger children all poked their tongues out at Mrs Ridgeway, who made a perfect 'O' with her mouth in disgust.

A bend in the road was coming up and Raymond didn't have time to slow down — he didn't really know how to, as he had only used one gear to go through the paddocks on the farm. At speed, he tried to steer around the bend, but the 1924 Dodge converted to a utility was not built for racing on dusty roads. It slewed sideways and into the drain on the side of the road, bouncing hard over it and into the scrub. He applied the brakes and the Dodge chugged to a stall. Raymond looked around. Everyone had white faces, looking shocked at this near miss.

Reverend Thomas tooted as he drove the Ridgeways by in their Packard. They all sat still in the car for several minutes.

'We had better get home,' said Eunice.

'Yeah,' said Raymond. 'Let's not go ute racing again for a while, OK?'

'OK by me,' said Eunice, getting her colour back.

The 1924 Dodge had lost half of its tray. The suspension was strained beyond belief and they had a flat tyre. They limped home and put it in the shed. Going inside to see their mother, they found their father John sitting beside her, on a chair near her bed. He stood and they all gaped at him.

'Hi, kids! Surprise!' he said. 'Have you looked after the Dodge for me?'

Let's not go ute racing again

for a while, OK?

Riley's Wedding (Funeral?)

RILEY STOOD IN FRONT OF the congregation and peered from face to face. His bride's family, on one side, glared darkly back. And there on the other side was his mother, wringing her fingers like they were live snakes that needed to be dead. And there was his father, whose hand she held, head down and snoozing in the pew, regardless. And there was his Shirl in her bridal kit in a chair by the altar, where someone had kindly stuck her to stop her falling over. She looked like a fried egg, he thought tenderly, all the crinkly bits spread around the plate; almost like a roll of dunny paper that had got wet on one end. He supposed her legs had got tired from all that standing up.

'I know I'm late ...' he began. 'But it weren't my fault, see?'

Shirl's family had done their best to talk her out of getting wed; she was such an elegant cook, which he figured came directly from being the ex-ex-girlfriend of the manager of the greasy spoon in town. But now that they were finally here, they'd changed their minds completely. They looked very committed. Riley began again, by apologising.

'I'm sorry. It were Bluey's fault I'm late ...'

'Bluey's bloody dead!' shouted someone from the back. 'Dead as a bloody doorknob, so ya can't blame him.'

'We wanna know why you kept our Shirley waiting. Yer should be bloody ashamed!' That came from Shirl's brother, who'd always been known as Muhammad Ali, and not for religious reasons.

The whole church shifted like a pie-bag full of blowies. Riley shuffled his feet.

'It weren't my fault, I'm telling ya,' he tried again.

'You'd better make this good,' warned Shirl's father, known far and wide as Rod for his inflexibility and the length of his one good arm. It was said that Bluey had been his only true friend. He'd tried to save his life that night when he tipped into the brewery vat, where he'd gone for a sly nog when he was thirsty. Rod had told him to try to drink the stuff, to save him. It was said he'd never recovered from the fact it hadn't worked.

Riley watched Ma try to wrench the heads off all of Pa's fingers.

'Well, you know how Bluey left his ute to Rod when he died?' He didn't really want to bring it up, but he knew he had no choice. It was another sore point. Rod had decided he seriously didn't desire it and had given it to Riley as a pre-nuptial present. Riley hadn't hungered for it either, but it had been impossible to refuse. ('Don't look a gift-horse in the mouth,' Rod had said. 'I WANT you to have it.')

'And you know how that mutt of Bluey's thought the ute was really his ...?'

They'd been inseparable, all three of them: Bluey, the ute, the dog. Riley looked around at eyes sharp as razors, especially on the bride's side of the church. 'That wasn't the worst of it. The worst of it was that the dog thought the new driver was really his as well.'

'Perhaps I'd better start at the very beginning,' said Riley, solemnly. 'I met Shirl at the butcher's when I went in for sausages. Shirl came round and showed me how to do sausages and it went on from there. Then one day she reckoned we should get hitched,' Riley gulped.

'Anyway, she still had the frock, see, from when Harvey Wilson did his runner, and she still fits it, even after the first baby ...' He took a deep breath. 'Well, anyway, things were fine, things were just dandy, until that rotten Bluey up and *died*.'

'I tell you, Bluey was like a brother to me!' yelled a bloke from the second row. 'You blinkin' watch yerself, I blinkin' well miss him.'

'Of course you do,' Riley said hastily. 'We all do, mate. And that's where that moth-eaten, weather-beaten, rotten excuse for a huhu grub comes in.'

'Yer won't speak ill of the dead or I'll yank yer tonsils out!'

'I weren't speaking about Bluey,' Riley offered quickly. 'I were speaking about the dog.' His shoulders slumped. 'If you could call that slobbering hand-grenade a *dog*. He won't get off the ute, y'see. He's claimed that flatbed like it's a boat and he's captain of the ship. He thinks he's the admiral!' Riley's voice got high.

'He does his exercise like a prisoner going round and round the yard. The *execution* yard. He pees off the back whenever the urge takes him; never seen a dog do that before. I have to park that ute two foot from the kerb or else he *wees* on people's feet when they come up to pat him.'

'Yes, well,' he shuddered, as though the memory made him truly distraught. 'Do you know, that dog can stick his tongue round the side of the vehicle and straight in the driver's ear? No? I think Bluey was bent if you ask me,' said Riley. He looked up guiltily, and continued when no one argued.

'Every night, round nine o'clock, he starts to howl. Stone the crows, you wouldn't believe it. Bluey'd be knackered, see, and just about to head to bed, and the wife, she'd be getting set for a quiet night, when the dog would start. Bluey would have to go shut the mongrel up, and by the time he got back his old girl would be snoring ... The dog kept 'em apart for years.'

'You'd have thought a dog wouldn't mind a sheila like Shirl who could cook, now, wouldn't you? But, oh no. That rotten dog hates Shirl's bones. Don't he, love?'

The bride, sitting in the centre of the fried egg, nodded sagely. 'I've never known a dog to hate no one as much as he does my Shirl. He thinks you're about as presentable as a dead rat on a dinner-plate, don't he, darl?'

The bowed head bobbed again, with a little more vigour this time. Riley got ready to sum up for the jury.

'So. We can't get that dog off the ute and we can't take the ute anywhere *without* the ugly mongrel. And when the son-of-a-bitch swallowed the keys, just as I was coming here early,' Riley stressed, 'pulled them out of the ignition and swallowed the damn things whole, there was nothing I could do except leave the ute parked, and him in it … At least I don't have to lock it — a man'd be a fool to take that dog …' His voice petered right away to nothing.

'Anyway, I went to get my mobile out, to call up old Seesaw to come and get me, and I couldn't find it. Then it turns out that the dog found the phone on the ute seat, and ate it as well! I had no choice,' said Riley, sincerely. 'I had no flipping choice but to walk the whole way here, the whole twelve miles.'

A hush descended upon the congregation, and there was not a dry eye in the house as every man, woman and child, on both sides of the church, acknowledged poor Riley's pain. He'd won that mobile for breaking in the biggest bag of balls in the Wallawalla rodeo, the invincible Attila the Hun. Only the bull had got pretty feisty and broken his as well, and he'd had to take his steak and eggs standing for the next three months. Even the bride's rellies dropped their heads and gave Riley and his phone two minutes' respectful silence.

'And after the wedding,' he said loudly, to no one in particular, 'I intend to *give it back.*'

Rod with the long right arm leaned miserably into his wife when he realised it was something with four wheels, four legs and no rechargeable batteries that Riley had referred to.

The bride rose to her feet and Riley proudly took his place beside her at the altar, while from far, far away, in the following tremulous quiet, came the unmistakable sound of a rapturous and magnificent howling. And after that a lesser one like the sound of a cell-phone ringing.

We can't get that dog off the ute

and we can't take the ute anywhere

without the ugly mongrel.

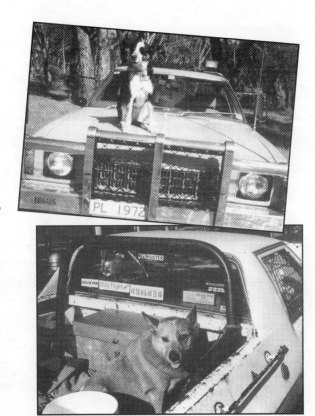

McEncrow's Hearse

WHEN WE'D BOUGHT HER, SHE was nearly new.

'What's 5000 kilometres?' Dad had asked. 'To the front gate and back.'

It may have been a bit of an exaggeration. But the house *was* over a kilometre from the nearest road, and connected to it by a road so deeply rutted that it would mercilessly tear out the diffs of townies stupid enough to brave the distance to attempt to sell us insurance or encyclopaedias. Once it ate the entire exhaust of an Avon lady, who then tried, unsuccessfully, to sue us for damages. We were saved by Dad's sign collection, which adorned the front gate. Mostly people didn't stop to read all of them. But Dad had once read about some meter man who sued a bloke because the bloke's blue heeler mistook him for a meat platter. Apparently the judge had ruled in the mauled man's favour, cautioning that a 'Beware of the Dog' sign would have saved the owner from litigation.

After that, Dad thought it prudent to err on the side of caution, and so our gate was festooned with a patchwork of warnings: 'Beware of the Dog, the Pig and the Wife', 'No Trespassing', 'Private road', and the 'No Hawkers or Canvassers' sign which had saved us from the Avon lady.

When the Council had finally straightened out Bent Back corner, Dad had acquired the 'Winding Road 3kms' sign and wired that on, too, by the holes left in it by twenty years of teenage target practice.

But my personal favourite was 'If we want religion, we'll come to you'.

So only the foolhardy or tenacious came to visit. Luckily our friends were both, and negotiated the perilous kilometre perched atop the ridges between the wheel ruts. You always heard the screaming of their gears before you saw them, as they worked the gearbox to slow their descent of the deceptively gentle-looking, but positively treacherous, hill above the house.

The ute had been a bargain, the likes of which are only found at deceased estate auctions. Dad reckoned you could halve a crowd and knock a quarter off the price of a house if the owner had died in it. But, in this case, the old bloke, McEncrow, had bundied off behind the wheel of the ute. The station hand had found the ute circling on full lock in the paddock. He'd seen some show, probably 'World's Most Stupid Stunts', and something retained from it by his less-than-sober brain had compelled him to jump, head-first, through the passenger window, thinking that the driver had just passed out and was in need of a bit of a hand. When he'd found McEncrow dead, he'd been so spooked he'd dived straight back out, leaving the vehicle circling while he hightailed it to the farmhouse to call the police. By the time they arrived three hours later, the ute was out of petrol and had stopped in the giant, doughnut-shaped wheel ruts.

Dad had stuck in heavy-duty springs to give her a bit of lift, and scraped a bit of road-kill off from under the bumper. We'd been wondering why it smelled like a Pal dog fart in there, but hadn't wanted to think about it too much. After all, the coroner had said that McEncrow had been dead for about a day, and it had been a scorcher.

And so, for nearly a year, we'd never really thought about the ute's former owner. She went well, received the same basic maintenance and quarterly hose-down that all the farm vehicles before her had been given, and had become just 'the new ute'. The old one was allowed to run out of rego, and became 'the farm ute' and the general paddock-basher.

The only reminder that we had of the ute's morbid past was the moniker that the blokes down at the local had nailed her with: 'McEncrow's Hearse'. Dad didn't pay much attention to that. He'd never been superstitious or religious, or so he kept telling us. And to date, I had to admit, the ute had given him no cause to start.

It had been one of Mum's clean-up days. Every so often, she got up Dad to do some maintenance close to home, and this time it happened to fall on the anniversary of McEncrow's death, though we didn't figure that out till later. We'd hosed out the ute, fixed the hen house and the vegie garden gate and mowed the house paddock. The grass had been brown on top where it had been scorched by the sun, but it was greener near the ground. Mum had an orphaned 'roo that she reckoned needed some green feed, so she got us to rake off the hay. In comparison with the hill paddocks, it looked like a bowling green when we'd finished. We sat on the verandah at dusk, smelling the new cut, watching the less-than-originally-baptised Skippy grazing contentedly, while we attempted to replace several of the litres of moisture that the sun had sucked out of us . . .

'Bloody vandals!'

I shot out of bed, not knowing what to think. I found Dad in his Y-fronts, gesticulating incomprehensibly, foaming at the mouth, and gesturing wildly towards the house paddock.

'Bloody kids! Nothing better to do! Deserve a good kick up the arse! Bugger!'

I looked. Two neat concentric circles deeply engraved in the paddock by some vehicle which, somehow, had not woken us, 20 metres away. This was wrong. But it wasn't the only thing, though at first I couldn't put my finger on what else it was that didn't seem quite right.

As the sleep drained from my brain, I knew. First, the circle was a clean ring. No entry or exit paths. And second, I'd padlocked the gate the night before. And even from 30 feet away, I could see that it was still intact. A chill shot up my spine. I headed for the shed. The ute, which I'd hosed off myself before garaging it, was encrusted to the dress rims with mud. The wheel arches were packed with clay. But it was the smell that got me — the unmistakable stench of long-dead road-kill.

Down at the pub, the locals were theorising.

'Crop circles.'

'Act of God.'

'McEncrow's ghost, mate.'

'Aliens.'

'Bloody big snails.'

'Mutant nematodes . . . I'll lend ya me sprayer.'

Dad downed another cold one, and told them for the tenth time that they were all stupid buggers.

But that night, as he stopped so I could open the gate, the ute's headlights hit a bald spot where my favourite sign had once been.

The only reminder that we had of the ute's morbid past was the moniker that the blokes down at the local had nailed her with: 'McEncrow's Hearse'.

Hot Rod

G'DAY. I'M A FISHERMAN. Well, I used to be a fisherman, but I kind of lost interest after I caught the biggest fish ever caught in Australia. I used to fish off the cliffs near here. When you're cliff fishing you use a rod to catch them, but when you get them to the base of the cliff you have to use a gaff on the end of a rope to bring them up. That's where my ute comes in.

You see, I'm a ute nut. I've been working on utes in my spare time since I was ten and couldn't undo the nuts on the tyres without jumping on the wheel brace. Well, my ute and me often used to go fishing. It's great to have the mates around to work on cars, but when I'm fishing I only need my car for company. I used to pretend she helped me land them because I tied the gaff rope to her towbar. Well, one day she did help me.

I had hauled up two or three fish, dragging them up the cliff with a three-hooked gaff on the end of a rope. Call me a perfectionist if you want to for using a 70-metre rope that could lift a bus, but I never wanted to lose a fish because a rope broke. The fourth fish I caught was a Spanish mackerel, good one, maybe 20 kilos. He fought but I finally hauled him to the base of the cliff and snagged him with the gaff. Then it happened.

Lifting the mackerel clear of the water I caught a movement off to the left, fast and gleaming like a mirror just below the surface, churning up the water like a speedboat and as long as a Jap mini-sub at the War Memorial. With a tail thrash that would have sunk a tinny it leaped out of the water and swallowed mackerel and gaff in one bite, landed with a splash that wet my boots 10 metres up and headed for the open ocean.

It's hard to keep a clear head in a situation like that but I managed. I turned and ran for the ute, jumped in, rammed my foot on the brake, checked it was in first gear and the handbrake was on, and waited. I didn't have to wait long. That fish ran out of rope with a jerk that pulled the ute back a metre and nearly gave me whiplash. Thank God the chassis was as strong as a tank's, or the towbar would have ripped clean off.

Anyway, I sat there expecting the rope to break and pushing down on the foot brake as hard as I could. The fish ran to the left and ran to the right and on the end of each run the jerk would pull the back end round but still that rope held.

After about three hours of this I was getting worried. My foot was aching, my legs were beginning to tremble and if I hadn't blown up my ex-girlfriend's inflatable neck collar and stuck it on I would have had a crook neck for months. The thing that was really pushing my panic buttons was that the fish had worked the ute back 15 metres till there was only a metre and a half left between the tailgate and the edge of the cliff.

I had a real problem. If I jumped clear I would save my life, but my ute would be smashed to pieces at the bottom of the cliff and the fish would get away. Even if my insurance company believed my story, I would never get back all the hours of work me and my mates had put into that ute. She was the shiniest, glossiest piece of mobile art from Perth to Cairns and she had the best-tuned, most powerful legal donk in the country. She had cost me thousands of dollars and two relationships but she was worth it. I had to stay with her to the end if that was the way it had to be.

I knew the fish was tiring, because the time between runs was getting longer. Bang! Another jerk and I was half a metre closer to the cliff. Two more of those and I would be a goner. I waited … and waited … Nothing. It was time to act.

Carefully I started the engine and waited for a response from the other end of the rope, but my baby snored so peacefully the fish didn't have any idea what it was up against. I eased off the handbrake, ready to haul it on again instantly. I eased off the foot brake, let the clutch out and gently moved forward. I could imagine that fish, half-asleep, too tired to feel the pain, drifting along slowly flapping its fins. Suddenly it noticed.

I had pulled slowly forward four metres when it started. The fight was on! That fish was awake and full of adrenaline. It tried to take off and it dragged me back a metre. I increased the pressure on the accelerator and held it with the tyres spinning and smoking and dirt and turf flying out from under me and over the cliff. The fish headed right, but the ruts I was making came in handy and at the end of this run I held my position.

When the fish stopped I increased the power again. The soil was shallow and I was down to the rock, so the tyres gripped and I began to haul the fish forward. I won't bore you with the details of how my ute, that fish and me struggled back and forth for another hour, but the fish really didn't have a chance against my baby. Eventually that giant head slid over the top of the cliff and into the history books.

When I had dragged it far enough over to make sure it couldn't flap back into the sea, I grabbed a baseball bat from the back of the ute and stunned it. Then I rang my mate Jeppa on the mobile and he came with his crane. When he saw the fish he called a television station, and soon there were helicopters landing all over the place with camera crews and pretty little reporters asking questions.

I was famous for a time and an American museum eventually bought the fish. It's amazing what people will pay for a 'freak of nature'. That's how I was able to set up my own museum, 'Newt's Classic Utes'. Most people who come in see the picture of the fish and me and think it's a fake. I see them laugh.

But some people remember the headlines, and if they're fishermen they ask, 'What kind of tackle did you use?' I just look at them and say, 'A climbing rope, a gaff, and that ute over there.'

Marty's Long Sleep

BLOODY GOOD FUN AT THEM B&S balls. Isn't it, eh?

You can get blotto, and you usually do, and you can get tired and want to sleep, and you usually do, and if you get lucky you can get a sheila, and you usually do!

Not Marty. Marty wasn't a lucky bastard. Marty was just a boozer, and an aggravating one at that. He drove an old HQ ute with a ratty old interior and 400 kilos of rubbish in the cabin.

A few years ago at the local B&S ball we were all there and in comes the mouth from the west clutching a stubby, and already he's talking crap. Well, what were we to do? This bloke would wind himself up on whatever he could find and latch on to your ear and hold on like a Jack Russell. Then he'd get stroppy and then get tired and want to go to sleep.

Well, this time he did it again, didn't he? And we were ready for him, weren't we?

At about half twelve he staggered off to his heap of rubbish and fell onto the seat and went to sleep. He slept and slept and slept and still had not surfaced at four the next day!

We had all been to the recovery party, dropped down a few cold ones and generally slouched around the place for a couple of hours and had a bit of a sleep, but still no Marty.

'I suppose we'd better go and see if he's still up at the recreation area where we left him. He could have choked or anything.' So off we goes. We opened the door of the ute and he was lying there awake, propped up on one elbow on the seat, his strides all wet from where he must have had a dream of going to the toilet and gone!

'Gees, it's been a long night, mate!' he said. 'I could have swore that I seen three o'clock go round twice!'

Well, he had, and by crikey, we'd got him a beauty, hadn't we?

When he arrived the day before and had started on his verbal diarrhoea, a couple of the mates had gone and painted all the windows of his ute MATT BLACK!! Marty hadn't noticed when he passed out in the front seat after midnight … sucked in, Marty! Serves you right you noisy bastard!

Bloody good fun at them

B&S balls. Isn't it, eh?

Thicker than a Brick

A COUPLE OF BLOKES WHO were not too smart drove their ute into a timber yard. One of them walked in the office and said, 'We need some four-bee-twos.'

The clerk said, 'You mean two-by-fours, don't you?'

The man said, 'I'll go check,' and went back to the ute.

He returned a minute later and said, 'Yeah, I meant two-bee-fours.'

'All right. How long do you need them?' The customer paused for a minute and said, 'Uh … I'd better go check.' He walked back to the ute.

After a while he returned to the office and said, 'A long time. We're gonna build a house.'

Big Al

BIG AL WAS A QUALIFIED plumber, as well as a qualified accountant, as well as a qualified electrician. All his life he suffered an addiction to studying. Whereas most blokes hated the thought of bending over the books, he just loved it. Maybe study was a way to escape from his wife, or maybe Big Al just had a Big Brain . . .

Anyway, Big Al decided to become the Most Complete Tradesman on planet earth. With all his qualifications he could clear a blocked toilet, rewire his electric eel, and take on the Tax Office when they disputed his depreciation allowance. He was a bit like the Cisco Kid, brandishing a variety of guns and ready to take on anyone, any time, any place.

Big Al was an orphan who desperately wanted to make good. Why, he hadn't even worn shoes until he was seventeen! To his delight his business flourished, but that was mainly because he was a hard worker. Even though he was studying law at night, he still put in his fifty hours a week bringing joy to the world as the best odd job tradesman in his town. His only limitation was that he was colour-blind, so he tended to steer away from electrical jobs that involved high voltage.

He wasn't very image-conscious, so he didn't care where he lived or what he drove. His accountant mates used to look down their snotty noses at Big Al as they streaked past in their Volvos and Saabs, because Big Al drove a cranky, smoky Valiant Wayfarer ute, painted red, with pretty large rust holes along the doors and sills. He consciously chose red when he bought the Wayfarer from the wrecker, because he knew that one day all the paint would match all the rust. His large brain was always looking years ahead, a fact that annoyed his wife and all his mates.

Another fact that annoyed his wife was that Big Al had off-road tyres fitted to the two passenger-side wheels of the ute, whereas he ran standard on-road tyres on the two driver-side wheels. He did this to make a subtle point to his wife, because she tended to drive a long way over on the left-hand side of the road, with the passenger-side wheels constantly running off the bitumen and into the gravel and dirt. It annoyed the heck out of Big Al, but he never actually mentioned it to her. He just gloated that he had solved yet another problem using that large brain that he was sure he had.

Big Al kept the Wayfarer a few kilometres ahead of a major breakdown, because he was also a pretty smick mechanic. He completed numerous mechanical short courses during the uni Christmas holidays each year, so he knew which end of a wrench to hold.

To the delight of his mates, Big Al had some weird habits. Like the day he bought the Wayfarer he chucked the keys out the window and into the bush while driving home. He then rigged up under the dash so he could quickly hot-wire the ute any time he wanted to start it. 'Keys wear holes in yer pockets, don't believe in 'em,' he'd tell the occasional cop who thought he was stealing the ute.

Another intriguing habit was Big Al's method of waking up in the morning. Between five and five-thirty every morning, Big Al would suddenly break wind. It was usually one sharp 'crack' that sounded like a .303 rifle shot. Almost simultaneous with his mega-fart, Big Al would sit bolt upright and scream, 'What was that?' He'd then climb into the shower as though this was normal behaviour. It scared the daylights out of Big Al's mates when they went camping.

All the Wayfarer's accessories were products of Big Al's fertile imagination. His large brain, coupled with his mechanical brilliance, had created a manic desire to make his working life as efficient as possible. He'd made a pair of steel ladder racks which, when the horizontal bars were unclipped, telescoped out to become the jibs of a pair of cranes. The jib cables ran to an electric yacht winch bolted to the tray just behind the cabin. A bank of batteries, which were fed by a Honda generator that sat in the tray, fed the electric winch. With the flick of a switch and a bit of juggling, Big Al used to boast to his mates that he could lift a year-old heifer off the ground and into his ute. This incredible set-up was actually what fuelled Big Al's 'agricultural disaster'.

It happened like this.

One time, when uni was in recess and there were no short courses available, Al decided to pack up his Wayfarer and go and do 'work experience' at a Taree dairy farm. While he was there he asked Farmer Bill heaps of intelligent questions, like: 'When a cow laughs does milk come out its nose?' and 'Is it hard to train the cows to run through the gate when the blue heeler barks?'

It had been raining a fair bit and it was really boggy around the milking sheds. A large, nasty-looking Friesian cow had wandered into the mud hole halfway down the paddock above the main shed, and got stuck up to her belly in the slop. Farmer Bill was about to get his Kubota tractor to try and pull her free, when Big Al said that he could do it quicker and easier with his ute.

Well, Big Al edged his way as close as he could to the bog hole, and swung his crane jibs towards the cow. With a lot of effort he got a wide sling around the cow, and tethered each end to a jib. With his Honda generator roaring flat-out, the winch grinding, both jibs straining, and the ute spinning its wheels, he started to pull the bellowing beast out of the mud. 'Leverage,' muttered Big Al as he sensed victory. To the amazement of Farmer Bill, his wife and their eight kids, it started to look like it was going to work, that the Wayfarer Ute was going to win — the cow would be free!

However, just when all the forces were at 'max', the two on-road tyres on the driver's side of the ute let go, causing the ute to skew sideways. The Wayfarer started to slowly slide in an arc downhill around the cow, and as it did the strap went slack. The yacht winch sensed the slack and sped up, causing the sling to reel in faster, which in turn accelerated the ute's slide. With the anchored cow acting as the fulcrum, the ute gathered speed and shot off at a tangent, like a comet escaping the gravitational pull of the earth.

Farmer and Mrs Bill gasped in horror as Big Al, crouching in the back of the ute at the controls of his winch and dual cranes, stared bug-eyed at the milking shed, which was approaching at the speed of light.

Big Al threw himself onto the floor of the ute just as the Wayfarer broadsided into the milking shed. The ute cleared away the first row of milking machines like ten pins, and then smashed side-on into the two-hundred thousand-litre milk storage vat. The impact was so great that the stainless steel vat was rocked off its concrete legs, went through the wall, and started off down the rain-soaked hill. Two hundred thousand litres of warm, high-fat, containerised milk headed straight for the main road, followed closely by one very bent Wayfarer ute. Big Al's teeth were clenched so tight a termite wouldn't have been able to fight its way into his gob!

To cut a painful story short, the vat hit the bitumen road and ruptured, sending a tidal wave of milk down Mrs Collis's hallway (she was a widow who lived opposite). Luckily, Mrs Collis was a good swimmer and liked milk.

Big Al woke up in John Hunter Hospital (without the sound of a .303) two days later, in traction, swathed in bandages and suffering from milk on the lungs. After Big Al had been lying there staring at the ceiling for half an hour, a nurse wandered in and saw he was conscious.

'How are we feeling today?' she asked with professional concern.

'Pretty bloody angry. The wife's never gonna drive me ute again. If she hadn't forced me to fit them mismatched tyres none of this would've happened . . . By the way, do ya run any courses in this place?'

Tips for Ute Lovers

UTE STICKER & PRODUCT CATALOGUE: Send stamped addressed envelope to Bluey's Ute World, 27 Rowood Rd, Prospect NSW 2148. Also see **www.blueys.com.au**

UTE PUB: Visit Australia's first Ute Drivers Pub at Korong Vale, Victoria and **www.utepub.com**

OUTBACK UTE ANNUAL: Ute blockbuster magazine available December 2001, call (02) 9908 8050 or email **outback@outbackmag.com.au**

UTE MUSTER: For best Ute Videos in the world visit **www.utemuster.com.au**

OPPORTUNITY INTERNATIONAL: Bluey's is donating part of the proceeds of this book to Opportunity International. Check out their website at **www.opportunityinternational.com.au** to learn about their fantastic self-help programs.